"Metes, Gundry, and Bradish have the prescription for the essential attribute of competitive organizations in the Networked Age. *Agile Networking* is a practical guide to all of us who are anxious to build personal competency as effective members or managers of virtual teams. For those of us who may not have inherited Agility in our personal or organizational DNA, this book tells us not only what we are missing, but how to get it."
—*Chris Brennan, Program Manager,*
Technology Supported Team Solutions, IBM

"The authors have brought together the two main themes of agility and networking in a coherent and persuasive way. The book succinctly describes and demonstrates—using real and well-constructed examples—the application of agile principles and the overlap and linkages to networking. This is a practical guide for anybody interested in applying some of the latest management thinking."
—*Phil Fearnley, Team Leader,*
Knowledge-Based Business, Ernst & Young

"*Agile Networking* makes a valuable and timely contribution to our understanding of organizational design."
—*Barton J. Goldenberg, President,*
Information Systems Marketing Inc.

"A first-rate contribution to how we should be thinking about organizational agility issues. From this important work, we understand that the agile organization is:

- *A*ction-oriented by nature
- *G*lobal in conceptual scope
- *I*ntelligent in execution
- *L*ean in organization
- *E*ntrepreneurial in spirit.

This book is both provocative and practical, and should be 'required reading' for those engaged in organizational development and change."

—*Frank A. Medeiros, Ph.D.,*
Associate Vice Chancellor Academic Affairs,
The California State University

"This book takes important steps to demystify the hype surrounding Knowledge Management and creates a clear perspective on how to gain true leverage from an organization's valued knowledge assets. Anyone considering the knowledge creation or learning system architecture of their business should read this book!"

—*Glen Tines, Strategic Change Services,*
Hewlett-Packard Company

"*Agile Networking* enables us to maximise what we have learned so far and place it within a new framework that will transform both internal and external relationships."

—*Tim Yorke, Strategic Change,*
Commercial Union Assurance Company plc

AGILE NETWORKING:

COMPETING THROUGH THE INTERNET AND INTRANETS

by
George Metes
President, Virtual Learning Systems, Inc.
Partner, Agility International

John Gundry
Director, Knowledge Ability Ltd.
Partner, Agility International

Paul Bradish
Associate Director, DMR Consulting Group

To join a Prentice Hall PTR Internet mailing list, point to: **http://www.prenhall.com/mail_lists/**

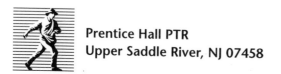

Prentice Hall PTR
Upper Saddle River, NJ 07458

ISBN 0-13-760125-5

9 780137 601257

90000

Editorial/production supervision: *James D. Gwyn*
Page layout: *Eileen Clark*
Acquisitions editor: *Michael M. Meehan*
Cover design director: *Jayne Conte*
Cover design: *Bruce Kenselaar*
Manufacturing manager: *Alexis R. Heydt*
Marketing Manager: *Stephen Solomon*
Editorial Assistant: *Bart Blanken*

 © 1998 by Prentice Hall PTR
Prentice-Hall, Inc.
A Simon & Schuster Company
Upper Saddle River, New Jersey 07458

Printed in the United States of America
10 9 8 7 6 5 4 3 2 1

ISBN 0-13-760125-5

Prentice-Hall International (UK) Limited, *London*
Prentice-Hall of Australia Pty. Limited, *Sydney*
Prentice-Hall Canada Inc., *Toronto*
Prentice-Hall Hispanoamericana, S.A., *Mexico*
Prentice-Hall of India Private Limited, *New Delhi*
Prentice-Hall of Japan, Inc., *Tokyo*
Simon & Schuster Asia Pte. Ltd., *Singapore*
Editora Prentice-Hall do Brasil, Ltda., *Rio de Janeiro*

CONTENTS

Part 3: AGILE OPERATIONS 129

Chapter 10
Agile Teaming 131

Chapter 11
Agile Learning Services 153

Chapter 12
Agile Law Services 175

Chapter 13
Agile Management 189

FOREWORD

"What Technology Is Doing To Us" is the cover page title for *The Sunday New York Times*—which I'm about to read. It struck me that a sub-title for *Agile Networking* might have been "What Technology Is Permitting Us To Do."

Metes, Gundry, and Bradish have provided those involved in a competitive environment with a taxonomy built on the work of The Agility Forum. The principles of agility are to: enrich the customers, master change, leverage all resources, and cooperate in order to compete. *Agile Networking* describes how to use Networking—the human side—so as to harness the capabilities available to, and within, an organization in order to react to unexpected change wherever it might originate.

The enhancement of group communications via networks—intranets, Internets, extranets, etc.—to obtain data and information in an agile manner so as to permit knowledge workers to respond quickly is thoroughly developed. What has to be done? What has to be managed? How to leverage the organization to be successful? Questions we all ask which are dealt with here in a rational, no-nonsense approach.

The implementation of an Agile Network permits an enterprise to react to, anticipate, and implement change. In fact, master change for greater efficiency and competitive advantage.

Everything is not nirvana. Some challenges do exist, i.e., legal services, commerce, education, etc., but these are the opportunities for those who undertake to master change before the competition.

—William "BJ" Johnson
Vice President, Networking Products Division
Compaq Computer Corporation
September 1997

PREFACE

Carpe diem! Carpe rete![1]

The core concept of *Agile Networking*—the union of agility with networking—represents a significant point in the evolution of 21st century organizational knowledge. This book combines new thinking about agility with tested knowledge of organizational networking in a language that describes the realities of today's business environment. Familiar topics such as change, teams, networking, intranets, knowledge work, and process design are related in new, systemic ways under the aegis of agility.

None of the componentry of the agile networking approach is new. Teams have been around since the days of Beowulf and the Three Musketeers. Ethnic groups and telemarketers have raised networking to a fine art. Medieval philosophers knew that in our world "change is the only constant." Knowledge work has always been better rewarded than physical labor. And while more often than not driven by failure, process improvement is what we've always called progress.

Agility is somewhat less familiar, especially in the sense we use it— an enterprise-wide strategy for being competitive in conditions of change.

1. Seize the day! Seize the net!

Agility is not our invention; it is an art and science that have evolved for the past half-dozen years under the auspices of The Agility Forum at Lehigh University in Pennsylvania.

Agility has a single focus: to provide strategic direction, a taxonomy, methodology and capabilities to help organizations to be competitive in the face of change. Founded on a solid set of principles, agility accepts the validity of a host of existing organizational tools: voice of the customer, virtual teaming, leveraging of technology, process redesign, and so on. Indeed, it uses these tools to further competitiveness in the face of change.

Networking, on the other hand, has broad applicability. The Internet has created a whole new spectrum of commerce, entertainment, and human connectivity. Communication systems support virtual work teams, schools, communities and worldwide interest groups. In *Agile Networking*, we focus on a single attribute of networking: its ability to implement agile processes. These may be human processes, business processes or technology processes; insofar as they enable agility, they fall into our field of discussion.

This book describes a synergistic relationship. We show how networking is entailed in achieving agility and how agility provides a strategic direction for networking. As a comprehensive set of business strategies, agility recruits widely among tools and processes, including networking. We demonstrate throughout this book that networking is a vital capability for the truly agile enterprise. Of course, other capabilities are required for agility. We summarize these here and indeed address them in our agility consulting, but they are not the focus of this book.

Reciprocally, networking gains strategic impetus from being harnessed in the cause of agility. Rather than being a technology-led capability, sometimes strategically orphaned, and often managed in a piecemeal manner, we show that networking is a major factor in tackling the business challenges of the millennium years. Thus, networking provides one of the "hows" for agility; agility provides one of the "whys" for networking.

We make no claim for completeness here: our model is the fractal, not the encyclopedia. We provide enough breadth in our approach to cover the essential scope of agile networking. And in key areas we will drill down to provide explicit examples and recommendations. But we know that there are no limits to depth, and usefulness, not completeness, will be our guide.

A last note. This book does not discuss the technical aspects of networking. It is about what you do with networks to make your enterprise thrive.

Structure of this Book

Part 1 is dedicated to an exposition of agility. We introduce the concept and describe where it came from and why it is of value. We then describe the key principles of agility and the component strategies, capabilities, and processes. We comment particularly on agile methodologies to capture the effects of change. Throughout, we indicate how the networking dimension, discussed later, contributes to agility.

Part 2 is principally about the networking capabilities—or processes—of the agile enterprise. We commence with a discussion of the congruence between networking and agility. In succeeding chapters we describe, in the agile context, group communication, intranet publishing and knowledge management.

Part 3 is about agile operations: essentially, the ways in which an organization's functions are transformed in the agile networking environment. We focus on a few particular functions in detail: training, teaming, legal, and management. From these detailed descriptions, we set the pattern for transforming other organizational functions through agile networking.

Part 4 addresses agile networking at the enterprise level. It shows how whole businesses are being transformed through agile networking. We discuss virtual organizations and alliances, then the rapidly growing electronic commerce sector, and finally education.

Our Readers

We believe that this book will be of value to three kinds of readers.

Agility practitioners will gain insights into the ways in which networking supports agile goals.

Networking and IS professionals will discover not only strategies for creating networking-based business capabilities, but also the strategic agile context in which those capabilities contribute to their enterprise's survival.

For the broad class of readers—senior officers, managers, and staff—we provide a road map of sustained competitiveness in the face of change achieved through today's networking tools.

Web Site Support

We will be providing ongoing support to this book through Agility International's web site at http://www.agility.co.uk/ai.

There[2] you will find materials that extend the content presented here. We shall include comments on the book, as well as relaying news from our readers of their experiences in agile networking. In particular, we shall maintain a register of relevant web-accessible documents, including the references cited here that are available on the web.

About the Authors

George Metes is President of Virtual Learning Systems, Inc., of Manchester, New Hampshire, a company that consults on virtual work, virtual organizations, and virtual learning. Previously he worked in education and systems integration and is the co-author of two books about networked, virtual organizations. He is also a Partner in Agility International, a virtual organization that provides international consulting and education on agility. He holds a Ph.D. in literature and linguistics from the University of Wisconsin. He can be reached at (email) geo92@aol.com, (phone) +1 603 624 9501.

John Gundry is Director and Principal Consultant of Knowledge Ability Ltd., of Malmesbury, UK. His company provides training, coaching, and consulting on networked communication, work, and learning. Previously, he worked in aerospace research, systems consulting, and organizational communications. He is also a Partner in Agility International. He holds a Ph.D. in psychology from the University of Reading. His coordinates are (email) gundry@knowab.co.uk, (phone) +44 1666 824644.

Paul Bradish is an Associate Director of the DMR Consulting Group, part of the Amdahl/Fujitsu group of companies. He leads a number of entrepreneurial ventures exploring innovative ways to solve customer problems. He also supports the DMR Future Business Lab, which is working with DMR clients to practically address knowledge management, electronic interaction, and new theories of work and working through strategy consulting and facilitation. He holds a LL.B. (Bachelor of Law) from the University of Reading. His coordinates are (email) Paul_Bradish@DMR.CA, (phone) +44 118 9269045.

---

2. We intend that this will remain the address of our web site. But should its address have to change, the site should be locatable by initiating a web-wide search on "Agility International" or "Agile Networking."

Clearly, the authors have wide backgrounds with a common focus. Therefore you will find that different chapters reveal different perspectives. Of course, that's reality. We hope that you find *Agile Networking* both instructive and suggestive and that reading this book is as satisfying to you as writing it was for us.

George Metes
Manchester, New Hampshire, USA

John Gundry
Malmesbury, Wiltshire, UK

Paul Bradish
Reading, Berkshire, UK

August 1997

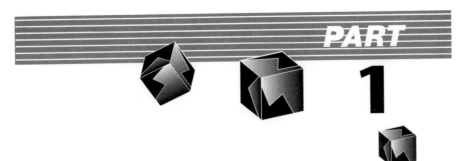

Agility

Since it is less familiar to readers than networking, agility will be our first point of discussion. In Chapter 1, we provide an overview of agility, putting it in the perspective of 21st century organizational realities. In Chapter 2, we step outside the usual industry organizational environment to help to illuminate key aspects of agility. We do this for a variety of reasons. Perhaps most important is that readers familiar with organizational processes need to be freed from the biases of prior knowledge. By moving into a different domain to explore agility, readers can appreciate agility as a system, rather than identifying with point solutions that they may recognize.

Chapters 3 and 4 are devoted to an overview of agility principles, those value statements that provide the rationale for agile processes. While there are only four basic principles, the implications of these principles justify an in-depth discussion.

Chapter 5, the final chapter of this section, describes the concept of agility change domains, a set of focused categories and methodologies that enables an organization to analyze its levels of agility in strategically important operations.

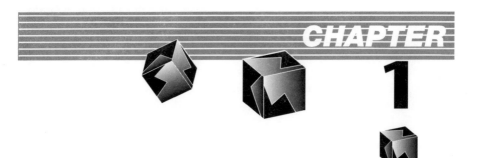

INTRODUCTION TO AGILITY

The rate of progress is such that an individual human being, of ordinary length of life, will be called upon to face novel situations which find no parallel in his past. The fixed person for the fixed duties, who in older societies was such a godsend, in the future will be a public danger.

—Alfred North Whitehead, 1925[1]

So as it was with professionals 75 years ago, so it is today with enterprises. Driven to compete in time, in an environment dominated by complexity and change, enterprises are desperately seeking the agility it takes to thrive. In this chapter we'll introduce the basic concepts of the formal practice of agility: what it is and why it's important.

Our principal sources for agility are *Agile Competitors and Virtual Organizations* by Steven Goldman, Roger Nagel, and Kenneth Preiss of The Agility Forum, published in 1995,[2] and the later book by these authors, *Cooperate to Compete.*[3] Also, we draw on an early Agility Forum report, *Key*

---

1. Alfred North Whitehead, *Science and the Modern World* (New York: Macmillan, 1925), p. 175.

2. Steven L. Goldman, Roger N. Nagel, and Kenneth Preiss, *Agile Competitors and Virtual Organizations* (New York: Van Nostrand Reinhold, 1995).

3. Kenneth Preiss, Steven L. Goldman, and Roger N. Nagel, *Cooperate to Compete* (New York: Van Nostrand Reinhold, 1996).

Need Areas for Integrating the Virtual Enterprise.[4] Our view of agility is based on these and other sources, as well as our own consulting experiences. Readers wanting a fuller, firsthand account of agility from its originators should study these and other materials from The Agility Forum.[5]

What Is Agility?

Agility is nothing less than an enterprise-wide response to an increasingly competitive and changing business environment. At its highest level, it is **an enterprise-wide strategy for being competitive in conditions of change**.

Agility is about being more competitive—creating the products and services that customers in a rapidly changing, fragmented, global marketplace will buy. While agility demands strategic responses from all parts of the enterprise—strategies that may seem far removed from directly affecting competitiveness—competitiveness in the face of change is its single guiding principle. Building customer databases, empowering people, working in teams, adopting new production methods, exploiting information technology, managing knowledge, creating quality missions, or forming virtual enterprises are all laudable activities; but they are not agility. As we shall see, agility involves all these things, and more, but only when they are strategically linked to a goal of competitiveness in the face of change.

Why We Need Agility

Commercial enterprises have always been competitive. Competitive success is behind the great corporations that we see today. Surely we know enough about competitiveness not to need another strategy?

The agility perspective is that competitiveness and success are not rights. They are earned through continually matching products and services to what the customer will buy. They are earned through continually responding to changes in the wider business environment. Successful enterprises evolve not through random mutation, but through purposeful strategies to respond to change.

4. *Key Need Areas for Integrating the Virtual Enterprise* (Bethlehem, PA: The Agility Forum, Report AR94-04, 1994).

5. The Agility Forum, 125 Goodman Drive, Bethlehem, PA 18015-3715, USA. The Agility Forum is home to a wide variety of agility-related information, case studies and examples, publications, resources, and training materials. It has also created a World Wide Web site giving visibility of and some access to these resources. Search for "Agility Forum" using any web-wide search engine.

Commentators will tell you that we are living through times of rapid change. Change is all around us, and the rate of change is increasing. What agility uniquely does is not only to recognize change, but to identify its impact on competitiveness and set out a strategy for mastering it across the enterprise.

Here are some examples of today's changes in the business environment that agility recognizes and masters.

1. Products[6] aren't what they used to be. Customers are eagerly accepting the individualized and customized goods that modern production technology allows and are rejecting mass-marketed goods. Consumer products and services now need to make a statement about individual life-styles—one size no longer fits all. Niche products are proliferating as markets fragment and economic order size decreases. Every business is now customer focused.

2. Neither are products and services amenable to a packaged, transactional approach. Supplier–customer business relationships are growing ever closer through just-in-time contracts, alliances, and shared-destiny partnerships. Business customers look keenly at how a product adds value to *their* customers. They want their problems solved, not to buy parts that they must configure into a solution. All customers now demand service quality.

3. Communications technology and especially the Internet have created new customer contact and distribution channels undreamed of, and largely unpredicted, as late as 1992. Internet-equipped customers can now browse your on-line catalogues as easily as anyone else's and make value-for-money comparisons. Internet now delivers information products regardless of geography.

4. Businesses operate in the global marketplace fueled by expanding communications and fewer political and tariff barriers. Companies are creating bridgeheads in overseas markets. Reciprocally, they see their marketplace under attack from overseas companies. Lines of authority on corporate organization charts now crisscross the globe. Companies must address new marketplaces and respond to new entrants in their marketplace.

6. Throughout this book we mean products to be both goods and services. When we mean to refer specifically to either goods or services, we say so.

5. Partnerships, alliances, and joint ventures proliferate. Companies that were competitors are now pooling their resources when needed R&D investments outstrip their individual capabilities. New markets are increasing the alliances and joint ventures needed to enter them. Companies are forging closer relationships along the supply chain to form virtual enterprises.

6. Knowledge is now regarded as a capital asset in its own right. "Knowledge management" is the buzz word of the late 1990s, as companies strive to place their intellectual capital under management remit. Knowledge about processes is now seen as a salable commodity. Information-rich products now proliferate, especially in developed markets. Commodity products are less and less profitable, because the skills for developing them have been successfully exported to low-wage economies.

This list highlights examples of the change taking place in the world of business as we write these words. In 3 years' time the list may be different. Here are some things that might just happen:

1. Increasing economic differentiation between the haves (employed, high-wage earners whose principal problem is managing time) and the have nots (unemployed or low-wage earners whose principal problem is managing money) lead to two marketplaces. Bespoke, craft, life-style-enhancing products for one market are unaffordable by the other, who will nonetheless buy education and entertainment products that the first market cannot find time to use.

2. Faith and religious belief create new international, pan-political alliances and communities that both open and close markets across the globe.

3. Ethical purchasing becomes more widespread.

4. Water and communications bandwidth become more important assets to a country than petroleum, minerals, and physical infrastructure.

5. New technologies—biotechnology and robotics—revolutionize production processes, making once expensive processes available to thousands of companies.

The point about these predictions is not that they will or will not be fulfilled; it's that the only thing we can count on is change. The only confident prediction that can be made about change is that it will accelerate. This is why agility is not about responding to *changes*, but having the capabilities and processes to respond to *unpredictable change*. Agility is about establishing the processes that allow an enterprise to master change from wherever it comes and however it appears. Consider a few of the associations we attach to the English word *agile*—outside its use here as a title for an enterprise strategy—as shown in Table 1–1. All these connotations of agile have to do with ability to change. In the physical sense, agility is about the speed of changing direction of movement, and its physical opposite is inertia. In the sense of mental processes, it is about the speed of incorporating new information: its best opposite here is ponderous. Agility is an intuitively appropriate word for this new strategy. What enterprise can be successful today if it is inert, lumbering, ponderous, and the like? Yet many of us have unhappy experiences of employers, suppliers, or legislatures who are just that.

Agile enterprises can be pictured as ballet dancers or basketball players, rather than marathon runners or weight lifters. Agility does not emphasize the stamina or strength of an enterprise per se, but rather its speed in redirecting its strength and its stamina to keep doing so.

Table 1–1 Some Synonyms and Antonyms for the Word Agile.

Words Associated with the English Word Agile	Words Having an Opposite Sense from Those Associated with Agile
Agility	Inertia
Brisk	Lumbering
Lively	Ponderous
Nimble	Clumsy
Supple	Stiff
Quick	Slow

But the agile enterprise does not master change for its own sake. It masters change so that it can create the products that customers value. And much of the change that it masters comes from competitive forces in the marketplace. Picture the Steve McQueen character's famous pursuit of a fleeing car through San Francisco's streets in the film *Bullitt*. At one and the same time, he's not only keeping the escaping car in sight as it hurtles down sidestreets and across junctions, but he's also dodging traffic and obstructions. Think of the escaping car as delivering products that customers will value in a changing marketplace and the traffic and obstructions as environmental changes to be mastered.

Where Did Agility Come From?

Agility grew from a report prepared for the U.S. Congress to identify ways of returning U.S. industry to global manufacturing competitiveness. Steven Goldman, Roger Nagel, and Kenneth Preiss, together with Rick Dove, an independent consultant, spent nine months in 1991 leading a team of manufacturing executives to create the landmark report *21st Century Manufacturing Enterprise Strategy.*[7]

Since then The Agility Forum, the operating name of the Agile Manufacturing Enterprise Forum at the Iacocca Institute, Lehigh University, has taken the leadership role in promoting agility. With U.S. government and industry funding, they have created a center of agility research, case studies, implementation, education, and awareness building. This has involved close association with industry in both steering group and direct participation roles, ensuring that agility directly relates to industry's needs.

At the same time the scope of agility has widened from manufacturing industry to commerce of all kinds. For example, in 1995 we developed independently in the United Kingdom an extensive picture of agility for the financial services industry. Later in this book we describe the application of agility in the educational world. Agility is relevant to anyone who has a customer.

---

7. Steven L. Goldman and Kenneth Preiss (eds); Roger N. Nagel and Rick Dove (principal investigators) *21st Century Manufacturing Enterprise Strategy: An Industry-led View* (Bethlehem, PA: Iacocca Institute, Lehigh University, 1991).

What Will Agility Do for Me?

Among the benefits that companies that have embraced agility report are the following:

- New markets for niche, customized products and services
- Long-term relationships with customers
- Faster concept to cash time
- Turning change into market opportunity
- Greater bottom-line impact of people, information, and technology
- Multiple win–win partnerships

Agility is for you if you want any of the following to describe your enterprise.

- You offer configurable, long-lived solutions based on need and value to the customer.
- Your customers see you as a long-term part of their business—and pay accordingly.
- You respond successfully to highly profitable windows of opportunity in the marketplace—and set the standard for all that follow.
- You are feared as the industry leader because of your ability to continually redefine the market, your offerings, and the rules of the game.
- Your name is synonymous with product leadership.
- You quickly and profitably bring to market 10 times more products than you can today.
- Seismic changes in the business environment that wreck your competitors leave you unscathed.
- When people first meet your company, they feel the buzz.
- You exploit all the best ideas that your employees, suppliers, and customers come up with.
- You rapidly get the right skills and knowledge applied to the right opportunities at the right time—and you never forget how.
- You quickly form multiple strategic alliances with foreign companies to open up international markets for joint products.
- Other companies continually approach you with attractive and realistic partnering propositions.

But who has done this and prospered? you may ask. Many enterprises across a variety of business and public service sectors, is the answer. Agility success stories are well documented by The Agility Forum and in the books from Forum authors already referenced. We see no useful purpose in repeating these success stories here. And they will be added to long after this book has gone to print. We strongly advise consultation of The Agility Forum materials to see who has done what, how, and with what success.

But it's instructive to look at how agile principles lie behind the avowed success of top business managers. In August 1996, *Business Week* magazine published as its cover story its list of the top 25 managers of 1995.[8] What made them top managers? *Business Week* explains the strategies that they used.

- They reshaped their companies to be more competitive.
- They led growth through product innovation, recognizing that the products that they sell are their main strategic asset. They saw the simple truth that fast growth was based on new products that customers wanted.
- They increased product cycles and created a greater diversity of products from existing lines.
- They didn't cut the business (downsize, or the like); they grew it. They grew it dramatically in the face of unprecedented change, intense competition, and global forces.
- They used corporate alliances to drive growth.
- They recognized the need to be global—forming partnerships in new marketplaces.

As we'll see later, the strategies of these successful top managers are encompassed by agility: focusing on competitiveness, diversifying products to delight customers, facing into change, and creating alliances and partnerships.

Let's look at the opposite. *Fortune* magazine in November 1994 contained a punchy article titled "Why Companies Fail".[9] Here's their list of six causes of corporate disaster.

1. Failure to concentrate on the fundamentals of the business: its core competencies, key goals, and reasons for profitability.

8. "The Top Managers of 1995," *Business Week*, August 1, 1996.
9. Kenneth Labich, "Why Companies Fail," *Fortune*, November 4, 1994.

2. Failure to anticipate and plan for change.

3. Alliances and stock injections that load the company with debt and decrease ability to change.

4. Resting on the laurels of past success, rather than concentrating on tomorrow's marketplace.

5. Failure to stay close to the customer and fast-changing customer trends.

6. Failure to build and sustain loyalty among the work force.

Agility would have helped companies that failed for any of these reasons. Agility, as we will see, draws attention to valuing core competencies, mastering change, focusing on the customer, and sustaining employee commitment.

None of the parallels between agility and *Business Week*'s success factors, and *Fortune*'s failure factors, should be surprising. As we have said, agility was created with the close involvement of industry. It's not a theory in search of data; it's a strategy built from experience.

Agile Principles

At its highest level, agility is an enterprise-wide strategy for being competitive in conditions of change. From that single proposition follows a logic of four principles and contributing strategies, capabilities, and processes. Agility is thus a coherent, integrated strategy of strategies—an encompassing vision for economic survival.

Agile Principle 1: Enriching the Customer

Enriching the customer means continually providing products and services that deliver value that customers will pay for. This principle anchors agility firmly in marketplace realities and the enterprise's economic survival.

Agile Principle 2: Mastering Change

In the face of continuous change, an enterprise that is to survive must master that change or be derailed. Change affects the enterprise from the changing needs of the marketplace, the greater variety of products that it must produce, changing customer relationships, and changes in the business, technological, societal, and legislative environment in which it operates.

Agile Principle 3: Leveraging Resources

In a competitive environment, an enterprise must leverage its resources to the full if it is to master change and enrich the customer. It cannot afford to have idle and underexploited resources.

Agile Principle 4: Cooperating to Compete

No enterprise's resources, however fully exploited, will be sufficient for it to enrich the customer and master change. The agile enterprise must regard partnerships, virtual organizations, and other types of alliance as preferred ways of extending its capabilities.

But agility is much more than simple statements of goodness. It involves strategic commitment to principles, an operational environment of agile processes built on agile technologies, and a culture of innovative people committed to further the enterprise's agile proficiencies. What makes agility so powerful is the detailed map of tested approaches that allow enterprises to move from these statements of principle to implementable strategies and buildable capabilities. We shall see more of this rich, integrated texture in the following chapters.

The Agile Mind-set

Through our summary of agility in the rest of Part 1, we aim to convey the agile mind-set. We highlight this here, because embracing this mind-set is a crucial part of being able to migrate to agility.

The key is a change in mind-set from instances to processes and from the short to the long term. Table 1–2 shows some of the things that the agile enterprise considers important, in comparison to those that the nonagile enterprise considers important. You will see these examples in the chapters that follow.

Because it is rooted in change, agility requires more than being concerned with instances and events that are closely coupled with the current situation. Thinking has to be moved up a level to consider how instances and events come about. Much of agility is about gaining proficiency in "hows," that is, processes, rather than "whats," or instances. Agility also requires a focus on the long term as well as the immediate—an increase in the enterprise's attention span. By taking a longer-term perspective on processes, the agile enterprise has powerful and robust way of creating the conditions in which any number of different "whats"—or instances—can be created when required to respond to change. This is the essence of agility.

Table 1–2 Agile and Nonagile concerns.

Nonagile Concerns	Agile Concerns
Goods and services	Value of solutions
Transactions with customers	Relationships with customer
Efficiency of operations	Reconfigurability of operations
Work-force skills	Work-force adaptability
Items of information	Information infrastructure
A change	Proficiency at change
Work to job descriptions	Entrepreneurship
Management control	Management coaching
Outcomes	Learning from outcomes
Items of skill and knowledge	Creating skill and knowledge
Partnerships	Proficiency at partnering

The Bottom Line

When are we agile enough? The answer is never. Agility is a continuous process, not an end state. The business environment will always change in unexpected ways. Competitors will always catch up with you. New markets will always appear. New products will continue to redefine markets, and customer expectations will always increase. We can alter the Duchess of Windsor's dictum here: "You can never be too rich or too thin."[10] You can also never be agile enough.

In this chapter we have given a very high level view of the *what* and *why* of agility. In the later chapters in this part we will begin to look at the *how*. Succeeding parts of this book, focusing on aspects of agile networking, will develop insights into how enterprises can create and sustain agility using today's networking technologies. But first, in order to provide some concrete context for agility, we offer a scenario that illustrates some of the principles we have just introduced.

10. Apocryphally, advice from the Duchess in the 1960s to a New York socialite.

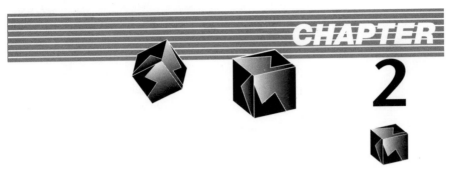

AGILITY IN ACTION

In preparing for battle I have always found that plans are useless, but planning is indispensable.

—Dwight D. Eisenhower, 1890–1969

This chapter illustrates agility through a metaphor with a military operation. We know that this may seem an odd inclusion in this book. However, we have found that this metaphor works very well in conveying an overall picture of the key ideas of agility.

We have selected a military analogy because many of the organizational arrangements, capabilities, and processes of a successful military unit demonstrate agility. Prosecuting the most extreme form of competition, military organizations have long taken for granted key elements of what we now call agility. Agility does not, however, require that an enterprise regard itself as at war with its competitors, however competitive their interaction in the marketplace. Nor do we applaud battle and bloodshed as desirable states of affairs.

The military scenario is informed by the experience of one of us in working as a consultant to the British Army some years ago. It may not be current nor correspond to the practices of other armies and is probably incomplete in many respects. The point of this chapter, however, is to illustrate agility, not military operations. The army described here, its opponent, and the tactical situation are, of course, entirely fictitious.

The Situation

To illustrate agility in action, we want to put the reader in the role of a colonel. You are in charge of the multiple direct assets of your regiment and the supporting assets of artillery, engineers, and so on. Your mission is to secure the relief of a small town in enemy possession. The surrounding area is held by the enemy. Your job is to deny them ownership of that territory and expel them from the town, minimizing casualties on all sides. The action takes place neither in your own nor your enemy's country.

Your regiment and its specialized supporting assets are the analogy for your company or enterprise. The town that you must relieve is the analogy of your customers. The enemy is the analogy of your competitors. The battlefield is the marketplace. The story takes place in the hours before a major battle.

The Hours before Battle

Planning for the Main Attack

Your planning for the relief of the town has been thorough. You have access to a wide variety of intelligence information about the physical terrain, the layout of the town, and the disposition of the enemy. Much of this information you received from headquarters, originating in the intelligence centers maintained by the defense forces. Modern communications meant that there was no difficulty getting it to you. From this information you have compiled an intelligence database and have drawn certain conclusions.

- Your principal strategy is to exploit a gap in the enemy's defensive position. They had established heavy battery positions around the town's perimeter, but your analysis was that their defended areas did not overlap fully. You knew that, while their senior officers believed that the whole perimeter was adequately defended, it would probably take them over an hour to relay the guns to cover those boundary areas. For an hour or so, therefore, there would be four or five corridors of relative safety through which to approach the town. If you could send fast-moving forces up those corridors, you could establish positions behind the enemy's perimeter, take out the battery positions from behind, and then secure the approaches to the town.

- You had spent time finding out where the power supplies and fuel reserves lay within the town. You also knew where the hospitals were and where the townsfolk were likely to shelter in the event of attack. You developed a plan for knocking out the power lines and fuel pipelines while minimizing damage to civilian areas, power stations, and fuel reserves. This involved your gunners in designing a new pattern of fire, which, much later, became widely taught at artillery school.

- In all this, you were enormously helped by a small resistance group of townsfolk who had been smuggled out and who were sitting alongside your planners.

- A particular tactic, through which you had rather made your name in your army career, was to mount continuous multiple attacks on the enemy from all fronts. Other commanders, you felt, operated too serial battle plans and did not organize their troops or logistics to be capable of switching rapidly from one operation to another. In your plan, many operations happened in parallel: the approach up the safe corridors, the attack on the power and fuel lines, and bombardments of the behind-the-lines positions, while all the time the main infantry forces were moving forward. Moreover, you gave your commanders on the ground considerable latitude to take the most effective course of action in the prevailing circumstances.

- You used your communications systems to advise all your battle and support units of this strategy. You considered the security risk of too wide information distribution, but decided that the battle could become so confused that there would not be time to issue intelligence updates on a need to know basis. Better that everyone had the full set and could assess it in the light of the specific situation that they encountered. In any case, the information was well protected by encoding systems.

Anticipating Damage

You knew that you would not get through this battle without sustaining some damage to yourself. There was the possibility that enemy low-level bombers could be mobilized from an airbase an hour away. If they did reach the battlefield, they would inflict considerable damage, especially as forecast high winds could prevent your air defense helicopters getting airborne.

It was just as well, you reflected, that your regiment was so well prepared to achieve its objectives in the face of damage and loss. So much of the structure and processes of the regiment in battle state was predicated on the reality of change.

- Chains of command could be dynamically reconfigured in mid-battle as command posts were temporarily or permanently lost. The sheer physical necessity for command posts to move was accommodated by duplication of resources so that one would be the center for command while the other was moving. Relatively simple rules governed complex and highly practiced routines for passing command to surviving command posts in the event of loss.
- Vital command and control information always continued to flow round the battlefield, always securely backed up and multiply reroutable in the event of damage to communication nodes. All the time, everywhere, commanders and soldiers had an up-to-date strategic and tactical picture.
- Commanders and soldiers were highly skilled in a range of battle operations through their peacetime training. Vastly complex arrangements for the objectives and disposition of troops, vehicles, and armaments could be conveyed and acted on speedily by reference to a few code words. Battle orders were preplanned and activated by the opening of secure orders. Battle scenarios themselves were highly refined: constantly simulated, modeled, and explored by the defense analysis experts; discussed and dissected at staff college; tested and practiced during exercises; and monitored and pored over by the operations research people to ensure effectiveness, robustness, and repeatability.
- There wasn't much about their equipment that your soldiers didn't understand. Each transmitter, computer, vehicle, tank, gun, and aircraft had been thoroughly exercised in all conditions for all its roles. The performance and characteristics of every electronic or mechani-

cal asset of the regiment were thoroughly understood and at the fingertips of each person responsible for it. Throughout your army each equipment worked in concert—fuel, armaments, and even data were interoperable. Highly complex but streamlined systems of maintenance ensured rapid recovery through first-line replacement of modular items and their subsequent repair at second-line and fall-back maintenance depots.

- And the soldiers themselves were the force that so supremely took all this capability into action. Their flexibility and resourcefulness under battle were not only a testament to their personal courage, but the result of years of personal development and cross-training in a variety of skills and situations. This not only produced soldiers with all the skills that you needed, but let everyone understand how they could best contribute to the regiment's success.
- And you realized that the last time you had been into action with your regiment, they had been equally prepared for a humanitarian refugee operation. Then, as now, the soldiers and equipment were equipped for an unforeseen set of challenges through their underlying adaptability and preparedness for change.

Your Opponent

As you considered your battle plan, you reflected on your opponent. He had nothing like as well trained and prepared an army, but he had many more soldiers and more firepower. And he had the advantage of defending rather than attacking. Were there chinks in his armor that you could exploit?

- First, he was slow to make decisions. Operating a highly centralized chain of command, it would take him longer than you to react to the battle. None of the lower-level units were permitted to take battle decisions; indeed, they knew so little about the prevailing strategy that it was probably wise that they did not. But the net result was delay and inaccuracy as reports, requests for orders, and commands were relayed verbally up multiple levels of command and down again. That's why he'd be slow at re-training his guns on the uncovered corridors.
- Another problem was that he couldn't rely on his soldiers. His was a conscript army, and the younger troops felt it was far better to survive somehow than to win: conditions wouldn't be much better either way

the battle went. The older soldiers maintained control through Draco-nian punishments for the slightest misdemeanor, and every individual had to look out for himself. Apart from groups who operated weap-onry together in the most mechanical way, teams were almost unheard of. And, of course, they trained together so infrequently that no one had any reason to trust or rely on his neighbor or to be able to anticipate what others were doing.

- And he was so cluttered. The need for commanders to appear impor-tant had meant that regiments had mushroomed in size. They couldn't move quickly, and feeding and supporting that bloated orga-nization in battle took up half its energies. Economically, it was a nightmare: everything the army consumed was provided late and poorly built and came at enormous cost to the state.
- It hadn't always been like that, you remembered. There was a time when your opponent's army was the envy of the world. Military prowess was valued in the society, and a recruit could count on some of the best military training in the world. But defeats by more adept and adaptable forces meant that soldiery had fallen out of favor. While the politicians still based their policies on the assumption of military supremacy, no one could quite remember why they had been the best army in the world nor how to pass those skills on to younger soldiers, let alone how to develop the skills needed for fighting today.

The Nonaligned Country

As you considered your opponent, you also considered the nonaligned country nearby. A few miles distant was the border to a country that had declared itself neutral. They would offer equal support and succor to either side. Was there a way to use them to your advantage?

You got the signals clerk to arrange a call back to your country's For-eign Office and spoke to a senior official. What were our relations with this nonaligned country, you asked? Would there be any basis for making an approach to them for help? You were somewhat surprised and rather pleased with the answer.

"Yes, colonel," was the reply. "We've been assessing that situation too. We've studied the risks and benefits of approaching them to forego their neutrality and throw their lot in with us. It's tricky, because we both have a lot to lose if we both fail. But they've expressed interest. Our prob-lem is to position this with them in the right way—they're very consensus minded. I don't think one person can make the decision to go with us. But with the right approach, they may jump. Of course, that requires us to get our government's approval and that itself will take time, but if we can engineer a government to government dialogue, I think they'll agree to throw their hand in with us."

"What are we offering?" you asked. "Well, they're worried about the refugee problem if the other side wins. There'll be thousands of people streaming over their border, and they can't handle that. They know that if we win that will not happen, and we're offering to take back the refugees that are already there. And they know that if we win we'll keep our word, which is more than they do about the other side."

Throughout the night, you received signals confirming the diplomatic activity. While you continued to refine your battle plans, you were at the same time in continuous contact with your Foreign Office. Eventually, you hammered out the deal. The neutrals had originally wanted access to a disputed border region as their part of the bargain, but your political analysts had already decided that that was not on offer. The deal was that they would help if they could, in return for help with the refugee situation. It was your job to work out the details with their chiefs of staff.

So you quickly established communications between your strategic planners and their opposite numbers in the nonaligned country. What did their help mean? What did you need? What was strategic? What could never be admitted in public? When would they have to act? Who was in charge locally? How could they be contacted? Hours of conversations took place simultaneously at multiple levels of seniority between your regimental command post and the neighboring military.

Eventually, a strategy was worked out. One of your aircraft would mysteriously suffer navigation failure and fly through the nonaligned country's territory, but it would not be intercepted. Acting on "wrong" coordinates, it would bomb a pipeline that supplied the water to the town you were relieving. With no water, the enemy could hold out for three days at most. You would wait that out and then offer a surrender. Their commanders would find that difficult to refuse for fear of mutiny from their disaffected conscripts, who would be faced with a meaningless battle. You would offer them fair treatment. Perhaps the battle could be won without a drop of blood being spilt.

The Agility Perspective

The preceding piece of fiction was designed to illustrate certain of the core concepts of agility. Not all the concepts are illustrated, and the parallels between a military operation and an enterprise's competitiveness can't be pushed too far before they snap. Nonetheless, there are significant parallels between an organization's planning for agility and our fictitious regiment attempting to relieve the town. We elaborate on these parallels next.

Planning for the Main Attack

These paragraphs illustrate the agile principle of *enriching the customer,* for which the agile mandate is to achieve competitive advantage through adding value to the customer through solutions not products. The analogies are shown in Table 2–1.

Table 2–1 How "Planning the Main Attack" Illustrates the Agile Principle of Enriching the Customer.

The Hours before Battle	Agility: Enriching the Customer
Concern to avoid collateral damage to the "customer" (the townsfolk) through careful targeting of fire.	A hallmark of agility is attention to the value of solutions, not simply the delivery of product. This means understanding how the customer benefits from your solution.
Battle plan based on intelligence data.	Gathering and analyzing customer data and making these data available throughout the organization are parts of agility. Without detailed customer data, the enterprise has no basis for deciding how to add value.
Finding a gap in the enemy's defenses and exploiting it through insight and intelligence, not raw power.	Discovering and exploiting a niche place in the market is one of the most important agile strategies. Memorably titled "sneakerization" by Goldman, Nagel, and Preiss,[a] this is about fragmenting marketplaces to find opportunities for high-value, high-margin products. The transformation of sneakers into high-priced trainers is a compelling example.

Table 2-1 How "Planning the Main Attack" Illustrates the Agile Principle of Enriching the Customer. *(continued)*

The Hours before Battle	Agility: Enriching the Customer
Devising a new pattern of fire later taught in artillery colleges.	An agile enterprise recognizes the information value of solutions.
Assistance from a group of townspeople.	Designing your solutions together with the customer enables the agile enterprise to maximize customer value.
Operating multiple actions on many fronts at the same time.	Organizing for multiple solution cycles, running concurrently, is a necessity for shrinking solution lifetimes and thus increasing the variety of market offerings.
Distributing information widely throughout your forces.	This again illustrates the agile practice of making information available throughout the enterprise, rather than hoarding it.

a. Steven L. Goldman, Roger N. Nagel, and Kenneth Preiss, *Agile Competitors and Virtual Organizations* (New York: Van Nostrand Reinhold, 1995).

Anticipating Damage

These paragraphs illustrate the agile principle of *mastering change*. This means the ability to continue to be competitive in the face of changing demands from customers and a changing business environment. Military operations are probably the best example of organizations based on the certainty of change. Table 2-2 draws out the analogy.

Table 2-2 How the "Anticipating Damage" Paragraphs Illustrate the Agile Principle of Mastering Change.

The Hours before Battle	Agility: Mastering Change
Military organization is based on anticipating change to the physical points of command, while maintaining the integrity of the command chain.	This illustrates recognizing change as a continuing fact of business life and setting in place capabilities to deal with it whenever and however it arises.

Table 2–2 How the "Anticipating Damage" Paragraphs Illustrate the Agile Principle of Mastering Change. *(continued)*

The Hours before Battle	Agility: Mastering Change
Command and control information always available and dynamically rerouted around lost nodes.	This refers to possessing a reconfigurable infrastructure that supports information concurrency. The necessary information for people throughout the enterprise to do their jobs is always available, regardless of where they are or what tools or platforms they use.
Skill in executing a range of battle operations that are prepracticed and pre-planned.	Reconfigurable operations is an agile strategy. It means investing in understanding the processes of the enterprise so well that they are "plug compatible" with each other, allowing new situations to be rapidly tackled without undue delay.
Battle scenarios simulated, modeled, dissected, tested, and piloted in exercises.	Reconfigurable operations need to be modeled, simulated, and planned so that there are no hiccups in their integration or execution when needed.
Thorough understanding of the performance and properties of every piece of tactical equipment. Interoperability between equipments and modular design to permit rapid repair.	Again, the reconfigurability of infrastructure. Having the key tools and systems well understood so that their behavior is predictable, and integration and reconfiguration are speedy. Achieved through modularization and standardized interfaces.
Adaptable, cross-trained soldiers.	A key agile capability is an adaptable work force. Mastering change means having a work force that is trained in multiple disciplines, can adopt new skills readily, and sees its own advantage in making the enterprise successful.

Your Opponent

These paragraphs illustrate, by means of the negative, the agile principle of *leveraging resources*. If the enterprise is to be competitive through enriching the customer and survive the slings and arrows of change in the business environment, every aspect of the enterprise needs to be considered as a potential asset: particularly people's skills and knowledge. Table 2–3 shows the parallels.

Table 2–3 How the Description of the Opponent Illustrates, by Means of the Negative, the Agile Principle of Leveraging Resources.

The Hours before Battle	Agility: Leveraging Resources
Speed of decision making.	Having all the resources in the enterprise working to win demands an entrepreneurial environment. This means streamlining decision-making by decentralizing management and removing layers of hierarchy. Consequently, individuals taking more autonomous decisions need to know the overall strategy and mission.
Empowerment and commitment of the opponent's soldiers.	Fully leveraging the work force means building commitment. Micromanagement and strict controls work against this. Moreover, people give of their best when they are explicitly rewarded for the value that they add.
Teamwork, or lack of it, in the opponent's forces.	Teams, and especially multifunctional teams, are more robust, productive, and often innovative organizational units than the individual and play a significant role in agility. But cultures of individualism and unaligned reward systems prevent teamwork.
Size of the opponent's regiments and the noncore operations. Practice of supplying noncore resources in-house.	Leveraging resources means identifying your core competencies (what your competitors would buy from you). Too many noncore competencies slow down the enterprise and prevent competition stimulating advantageous cost and technical progress. The agile practice is to operate a lean core with contingent resources purchased when needed.
Opponent's training deficiency and loss of training mission.	If part of an agile strategy for leveraging resources is identifying core competencies, the other part is bringing them under the remit of management and setting up development plans. But care is needed: what made the enterprise successful in the past is not necessarily what will make it successful in the future.

The Nonaligned Country

These final paragraphs illustrate the last of the four agile principles: *cooperating to compete*, as shown in Table 2–4. When the resources you need to be competitive are not to be found within your enterprise, then partnering should be a strategy of choice, not of last resort. To operate effectively, partnerships need concurrent virtual organization arrangements.

Table 2–4 How the Handling of the Nonaligned Country Illustrates the Agile Principle of Cooperating to Compete.

The Hours before Battle	Agility: Cooperating to Compete
Considering an approach to a nonaligned country.	A key agile strategy is readiness to partner if it makes sense.
Foreign Office preparatory study of nonaligned country (NAC).	In making partnering a strategy of choice, preparatory work is needed to develop a profile of possible partners and to plan how a win–win partnership could work.
Foreign Office recognition of consensus-minded nature of NAC.	Partnering, and especially international partnering, requires sensitivity to cultural differences. Other nations see fundamental constructs very differently from the West, for example, hierarchy and decision making.
Foreign Office building approach within own government.	Partnering strategies must involve generating commitment to partnering among all the stakeholders in the business.
Prepared position on whether NAC would have access to a disputed border region.	An agile strategy for ensuring proficiency in partnering is being sure yourself about the assets and intellectual property that you can and cannot share. Having these issues explicit and known beforehand builds confidence to enter into partnerships.
Establishing multilevel communications between own forces and the NAC forces to develop the details.	Operating a partnership means operating a virtual organization. Although real virtual organizations operate for months and possibly years, and not one night, the principle is of seamless electronically based, concurrent work among peers in all partner organizations.

The final outcome of the story, that maybe a way had been found to relieve the town without a battle taking place, hints at a final aspect of cooperating to compete—the value of constructing win–win relationships with your competitors.

Final Comments

Agility is about succeeding in a competitive, changing environment, and our metaphor here draws attention to the fact that military planning and capabilities also have that goal, although the rewards and penalties are more severe than in business life. But, as we said earlier, the point of this story was not to illustrate military operations—it was to illustrate agility. We hope that through this story the reader now has an appreciation at least of the principles and scope of agility. In the next chapters, we look at these in a more structured way.

Concluding this chapter on a somber note, here is a historian's account[1] of lack of agility on the battlefield. The context is the Flanders Campaign by the British Army in 1917.

> Tactics had been on a rather low level, and if there were those who said that nothing else was possible on the Western Front there were others who replied that Napoleon would have found a way. But the British in Flanders had no Napoleon. Planning could not have been more routine. Except at Messines and Cambari, surprise and deception were neglected. A date for each attack was decided upon. The staffs glanced at their maps and decided which divisions would participate. These were assembled at the front. Guns and supplies were brought forward. Zero hour was set. Lines were traced on the map showing the objectives. A bombardment softened up the defenses and completed the job of tipping the attacker's hand. Finally the assault brigades went over the top and walked directly into the prepared entrenched enemy. Thus France and England had fought the war for three years on the Western Front; and as to which leadership of the two allies was the more inept Hindenburg writes, "The Englishman was undoubtedly a less skillful opponent than his brother in arms. He did not understand how to control rapid changes in the situation. His methods were too rigid." But, he admits, they were indeed obstinate.

1. Leon Wolff, *In Flanders Fields–The 1917 Campaign* (New York: Ballantine Books, 1958), p. 239.

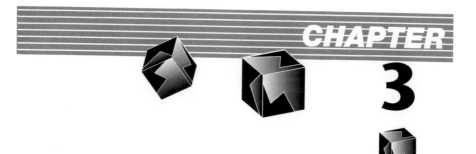

Agile Principles I

The agile principles are the set of core assumptions upon which the practice of agility is built. These principles extend as threads that connect and align the highest-level strategies of an enterprise with its lowest-level operations. For example, a company that includes in its mission "to enrich the customer" will operate through processes that enable the customer to let the company know what constitutes that enrichment, and it will reward employees for behavior that provides that enrichment. In this chapter we will first look at the first two enabling principles, enriching the customer and mastering change. In the context of each, we'll begin to suggest—at a very high level—ways in which enterprises can apply networking competencies to address each principle.

Agile Principle 1: Enriching the Customer

Enriching the customer means providing value to a customer through a solution, whose value is assessed by the customer, not the supplier. For a business customer, value means a positive impact on their customers—the customer's customer. For a private consumer, value means solving a problem or creating a positive psychological impact. In either case, enriching the customer is achieved by adopting a number of agile strategies and capabilities, which are described next.

Supply Valued Solutions, Not Products

Enriching the customer means providing solutions rather than products. This distinguishes agile solutions from mass-produced, standardized products suitable for times when rate of change in market demand was low. Furthermore, it distinguishes the agile domestic enterprise that has the opportunity and desire to engage closely with customers from foreign enterprises in low-wage economies who will continually force price down.

The value of the agile solution is measured by the impact on the customer, which in business regularly means the value added to the customer's customer. It is the customer, not the supplier, who assesses the value of the solution. Hence value pricing is consistent with agility. Consequently, internal quality mechanisms throughout the enterprise have to sense and be aligned with value as perceived by the customer.

Enrichment for business customers occurs when solutions solve problems for their business. Agility moves suppliers' mind-set from a focus on what outputs it is convenient for them to produce to what outcomes the customer needs to conduct business.

- Goods that enrich are cheaper, provided just in time, do not require further integration, fit a wider range of customer's products, and carry low managerial or maintenance overhead.
- Services that enrich require less management by the customer, are more fully integrated into their operations, and help to extend their business.
- Goods and services enrich when they form an integrated solution in which a physical element has a synergistic service element. The service element, regardless of its proportional cost, may become the basis of the customer's perception of value.

Agile solutions for private consumers regularly offer convenience. This is consistent with the pressures of an "attention economy," in which employed people's most limited resource is time. For example, disintermediation agents provide total solutions to personal management situations such as travel, house purchase, and even organizing marriages (less, generally, the selection of partner). The disintermediation agent is the sole point of contact for the consumer. It manages all arrangements that historically involved a variety of different merchants and service providers.

Offer Customized Products

Customization means a far greater focus on and provision for the customer as an individual, rather than as a statistical abstraction from mass-market survey data. Customization can itself be subdivided into different types, described as "the four faces of customization."[1]

1. *Mass customization*: the supplier conducts an explicit dialogue with individual customers to help them to articulate their needs.[2] (Agility goes further to identify that in business to business supply this is based on a close and long-lasting relationship.)

2. *Adaptive customization*: the supplier does not collaborate with the customer, but provides a product that customers can adapt to their requirements. (Agility particularly notes that many physical goods are increasingly platforms for information products that are highly customizable by the user.)

3. *Cosmetic customization*: the supplier offers a standard product in different forms to different customers, based on an understanding of how each customer wants the product to be packaged. (Agility notes this as one approach to market fragmentation, discussed later.)

4. *Transparent customization*: customers receive a customized product without knowing that it has been customized for them. The supplier obtains its knowledge of individual customers from its previous dealings with them, for example through loyalty programs.

Ten years ago, when working in the software industry, we were once told how futile it was to try to listen to customers, who either "don't know what they need, or all want something different." The lesson is clear: today they do know what they want, and, yes, they may all want something different, but that's the business's problem, not the customers'.

1. James H. Gilmore and B. Joseph Pine II, "Customization—The Four Faces," *Harvard Business Review*, January-February 1997, pp. 91–101.

2. In summer 1997, the Hewlett–Packard company advertised its build-to-order program in the UK press. They promised to deliver a personal computer configured to the customer's requirements from over 4,000 possible configurations in 48 hours.

Offer Niche Products

Closely aligned to customization, and a hallmark of enriching the customer, is creating market niches. This means actively seeking new products that fragment existing markets and then expand those fragments' revenues. In their first agility book,[3] Steven Goldman and colleagues coined the memorable word *sneakerization* to describe niche market development. This term derives from the transformation of sneakers from low-cost utility sports wear to high-price, multiple-purchase fashion items.

Niche products are typically those whose ownership makes a positive life-style statement. Fashion clothing is the most powerful example,[4] but life-style marketing is also used for food and beverages, entertainment and especially recorded music, self-improvement products, and even computer products. For the consumer of products this is good; for the easily overwhelmed, it's like Mozart's music was to royalty: "too many notes."

Collaborate with the Customer

This agile strategy underpins those already mentioned. Agile suppliers must collaborate closely with business customers if they are to know how to offer a solution and the value that the customer places on that solution. Indeed, truly agile solutions are developed in collaboration with the customer. Such collaboration is likely to be based on long-term relationships rather than brief transactions. It is likely to involve many people in both enterprises in close, peer-to-peer collaboration over an extended period. In *Cooperate to Compete,*[5] Preiss and colleagues describe the "enrichment," "reward," and "linkage" dimensions of an agile enterprise's relationship with its customers. They make the point that greatest enrichment of the customer, resulting in greatest rewards for the supplier, only comes about when there is greatest linkage (that is, the strongest and most cooperative relationships) between the supplier and customer.

Shorten Time to Market

Two further aspects of enriching the customer are related to time. Again, this rush to availability is driven by customer demand, not by supply side

3. Steven L. Goldman, Roger N. Nagel, and Kenneth Preiss, *Agile Competitors and Virtual Organizations* (New York: Van Nostrand Reinhold, 1995).

4. Indeed, the fashion clothing industry is an exemplar of enriching the (private) customer.

5. Kenneth Preiss, Steven L. Goldman, and Roger N. Nagel, *Cooperate to Compete* (New York: Van Nostrand Reinhold, 1996).

efficiency. Indeed, the issue is timeliness rather than speed; but since customers value faster satisfaction rather than slower, this resolves to new pressures on reducing times to market. Put briefly:

- The lifetimes of agile solutions are short. They are short because solutions have to be up to date in a rapidly changing marketplace and short because customers' requirements will be continually changing. Hence an agile supplier produces a greater variety of product every year than a nonagile supplier.
- Enriching the customer requires responding to the customer's time scale rather than the supplier's. When solutions are part of the customer's business cycle, value depends on their being delivered on time. When consumer goods are customized, conducting a dialogue about the upcoming product raises expectations of the anticipated benefit. A long wait for the product itself spells disappointment and perhaps cancellation of the order.

The Networking Dimension

The strategies for enriching the customer just described depend on an interrelated set of lower-level capabilities and processes. We do not describe all of these here. Here our attention is the support offered to enriching the customer by networking capabilities.

The agility literature cited earlier includes networks in its scope. Indeed, agility grew out of the seminal paper *21st Century Manufacturing Enterprise Strategy,* which introduced the notion of a wide-area network providing an infrastructure for supporting virtual manufacturing organizations.[6]

Here we extend the concept of network to networking and link networking competencies to success in the various dimensions of agility. In laying out these networking capabilities in relation to each of the four principles of agility, we form the link between agility and networking. This section can be thought of as describing the overlap of two circles: one circle being agility and the other being networking. The remainder of this book will attend to each of these networking capabilities in more detail, here we show why they are entailed in achieving agility.

---

6. Roger Nagel and Rick Dove, *21st Century Manufacturing Enterprise Strategy* (Bethlehem, PA: Iacocca Institute, Lehigh University, 1991).

Collaboration with the Customer

Networks offer great opportunities for collaborating with the customer. The best agile supplier is rarely in the same street as its customer. Networking—particularly use of the Internet—permits this type of collaboration regardless of distance. Networks are therefore vehicles for the types of linkages that enable agility. The bandwidth of the Internet and the capabilities of Internet tools mean, moreover, that customer collaboration need not be restricted to text messages between individuals. Prototype or product illustrations, plans, and detailed schedules can be exchanged in seconds. Groups of supplier and customer personnel can collaborate, regardless of distance, to create products. We talk about this type of collaboration in Chapter 7.

Collaboration with Other Suppliers

An agile supplier may be assembling its solution from goods and services provided by other suppliers. To meet the end customer's needs for solutions that fit and are on time, this supplier is likely to need close, network-enabled collaboration with its own suppliers.

A similar situation is when an end customer assembles a group of peer suppliers to work together to create a solution. This form of virtual enterprise is grounded in networks allowing continuous communication, regardless of distance, among all members. Such arrangements are common when knowledge and consulting services are supplied. Instant communications using groupware allow the best resources to work together worldwide.

Finally, aggregation, or arrangements in which a single agent seeks to replace multiple agents in a solution chain, typically involves Internet-based, fast-response networks. Aggregators are described in the context of agile networked alliances in Chapter 14.

Customer Data and Market Sensing

To customize a product or define a market niche, an agile supplier needs volume data about customer markets. Traditionally, market data are obtained from surveys and records of existing customers. In the networked age, a new source of customer data has appeared. Many companies now present their offerings on Internet World Wide Web pages. This provides a service for the potential customer, who can view detailed information about the product. In return, many companies now require registration before allowing access to their detailed information. Registration provides the supplier with information about the people who have enough interest in their product to spend time reading about it. It is as if a magazine advertisement could tell the advertiser about everyone who read their copy.

Internet offers another, but less direct way, to sense markets. Internet provides a window into different social and regional cultures. For example, a company selling a boating product in the Far East can learn a lot about its marketplace from the web pages of Japanese yacht clubs. The same is true for business markets. Small firms without marketing departments can get a rapid appreciation of the market for their products—and potential contact addresses—by browsing company web pages.

Sensing customer data and markets is discussed generally in Part 2, and, in the specific case of agile electronic commerce, in Chapter 15.

Delivery of Knowledge Product
Internet also offers a way to deliver knowledge and information products. A consulting firm can send its reports to clients a continent away using the Internet. Software companies can deliver their product as downloadable files upon receipt of a credit card number and retain detailed information about the purchaser. We touch on this in Chapter 15.

The Bottom Line

Enriching the customer needs to be a driving strategy for modern corporations. Customers know they can get what they need, if not from you, from someone else. Companies that thrive will be those who execute strategies to offer rapid, customized solutions or niche products whose price depends more on customer-perceived value or fit with life-style than the cost of production or other perceived supply side value. We've hinted at how networking can help you to develop the agility needed to enrich your customers; in later chapters we'll get into the nuts and bolts of developing these agile networking competencies.

Agile Principle 2: Mastering Change

In the face of continuous change, an enterprise that is to survive needs the capability to anticipate and master that change, not just react to it. That change arises from the following:

1. The greater variety and turnover of products that the agile supplier must produce, more rapidly, in customer-defined lot sizes.

2. The changing and uncertain nature of the business, technological, societal, and legislative environments in which it operates.

The strategies for mastering change fall into two camps, those to do with the operations of an enterprise and those to do with its people.

Have Readily Reconfigurable Operations

Agile enterprises face the challenge of producing a greater diversity of products than ever before, to the shorter lead times driven by customization and changing market niches, and in lot sizes determined by the customer. Thus the agile supplier must be able to reconfigure its operations easily and rapidly: easily, insofar as the reconfiguration must be robust and its cost viable, and rapidly, insofar as it must meet market or customer-driven time scales.

The Agility Forum uses the expressive term *plug compatible* to exemplify reconfigurable operations. Readily reconfigurable operations require reconfigurable processes, reconfigurable infrastructure, an adaptable work force, and information accessible everywhere.

Readily Reconfigurable Processes

To be readily reconfigurable, the enterprise's processes need to be modeled and then modularized.

- Process modeling allows planners to view, experiment with, and, in some models, simulate different arrangements of processes. From the point of view of reconfigurability, knowing about how processes fit together is as important as knowing about the processes themselves. A process model also forms a common basis for discussion about how processes can be rearranged.
- A process model indicates opportunities for modularizing processes. Modularization designs each process to be defragmented organizationally and to present standard forms of input and output to the processes with which it interacts.

Processes need, of course, to remain modularized to be reconfigurable. The goal is not to create a certain configuration of processes, but to increase processes' ability to be plug compatible to meet ever-changing product requirements.

Readily Reconfigurable Infrastructure

An enterprise's infrastructure represents a challenge to reconfigurability. This is particularly because infrastructure is associated with plant and buildings whose capability for change is low. However, reconfigurable processes will be hamstrung when tied to unreconfigurable infrastructure. In the same way that processes need to be modeled and then modularized, so does infrastructure, with the same goal of achieving plug compatibility.

An Adaptable Work Force

Reconfigurable operations depend as much on an adaptable work force as they do on reconfigurable processes and infrastructure. An adaptable work force can and will set down old practices, learn new practices, and adopt them in creating a greater diversity of product. Enablers for an adaptable work force are organizational units built round teams rather than departments, effective training, and compensation systems based visibly on the value added rather than adherence to a job description.

Information Accessible Everywhere

Having information accessible throughout the enterprise avoids reconfigurability roadblocks. Delays in establishing the information resources that processes require are avoided. This applies most importantly to the information that people need for their jobs. This is not only information about procedures or methods, but also information about customers, markets, and the rest of the enterprise. If information is to be accessible everywhere, people have to know where is it and be able to access it and apply it to their work.

Ubiquitous information accessibility is important for agility for two additional reasons:

1. Providing information across the enterprise is necessary (but not sufficient) for individuals and teams, wherever they are, to operate entrepreneurially (see the section "Leveraging Resources" in Chapter 4).

2. An agile supplier seeks to add *information extensions* to its goods, and thus information itself becomes an important part of a product.

Respond Rapidly

Being able to respond rapidly is an agile enterprise's response to both the changes in its marketplace and in its wider business environment. There are three elements of responding rapidly: concurrent operations, reduced cycle time, and rapid decision making.

Concurrent Operations

Concurrency requires taking operations that were once serial and making them parallel. In this way, the overall time to complete all operations is reduced. The risk that concurrent operations will diverge rather than converge is reduced by setting up intense communication between them. People conducting these operations must be willing to share and accept less than complete information—to work more flexibly with less certain data. Hence concurrent operations require an adaptable work force.

Reduced Cycle Time

Reduced cycle time is the recognized response for responding rapidly and is important for agility, as for any other business-improvement paradigm. Process acceleration is accomplished using modeling and reengineering techniques. Agility maintains that in reengineering processes the value of the process improvement to the customer is the vital criterion. A shortened cycle time that results in product defects or a less complete solution is unlikely to improve customer value.

Rapid Decision Making

Rapid decision making is a hallmark of the agile enterprise. Delays in management decisions can swamp any acceleration achieved by concurrent operations and reduced cycle time. An agile enterprise will consciously organize for rapid decision making through decentralizing management processes and speeding up information exchange. It will strive constantly to adapt its structure to that which is most effective for making speedy decisions.

Embrace Change

So far we have talked about mastering change in a rather cold-blooded way, concentrating on processes and operations. We have not yet talked about internalizing the need for change. All the changes in the world can (and will) be taking place in the agile enterprise's markets and business environment. Yet none will affect the enterprise unless it decides to do something about them.

Culture of Change as Opportunity

A strategy of embracing change must be driven by the most senior officers in the enterprise. They must proclaim that the enterprise's survivability depends on its ability to master change, and then act and be seen to act accordingly. They must help people to see that change represents opportunity, not threat, and then act and be seen to act accordingly. Everyone in the enterprise needs to understand this message, and it must be set by example by the most senior people. But there is also a role for comprehensive communications with the work force and work force education in entrepreneurship, discussed later.

Management itself must also explicitly explore and anticipate change and plan and practice responses. Scenarios, games, and simulations are useful methods. For example, six months before the collapse of world oil prices in 1986 the Group Planning function of the Royal Dutch/Shell company had managers explore a fictional scenario on just that premise.[7]

Change Proficiency Function

A change proficiency function ensures that the enterprise's ability to change becomes a recognized function. As a recognized function, it is placed under management remit, has budget and reporting lines, delivers solutions, and creates its quality metrics, just as any other organizational function. A change proficiency function works with operational managers to enable the reconfigurability described previously. It therefore needs access to modeling, reengineering, and change management skills, as well as close links to human resources functions. Because its principal task is to make the organization proficient at change, it must be a center for organizational learning about change.

Entrepreneurial Environment

We said earlier in this chapter that continuing change will be a fact of future business life. Whether the enterprise does respond to change depends more than anything else on individuals' behavior. Whatever policies for creating a culture of change, or a change proficiency function, are in place, it is individuals who will determine whether the enterprise senses and responds to change. Such behavior is fostered by an entrepreneurial environment. Individuals in an entrepreneurial environment will

- Want to create and sustain relationships with the customer in order to better understand the customer's requirements and thus sell more and better solutions.

7. Cited in Peter Senge, *The Fifth Discipline* (New York: Doubleday/Currency, 1990), p. 181.

- Readily understand that the value of solutions is determined by the customer and not by the supplier.
- Make it their business to sense and interact with the marketplace both locally and worldwide, seeking new opportunities.
- Readily accept the idea of change as opportunity.
- Jostle and compete with each other, and cooperate with each other, to fulfill opportunities.
- Continually create new ideas and proposals for both products and process improvements.
- Have scant regard for the status quo, focusing on the future rather than the past.
- Make their own decisions and ask for forgiveness later, in preference to handing decisions up the line.

In the logic of agility, creating an entrepreneurial environment is a strategy that contributes to two agile principles: mastering change, described here, and leveraging resources. We will therefore say more about this in Chapter 4.

The Networking Dimension

Many lower-level capabilities contribute to the agile strategies for mastering change. Certain of these depend crucially on networks and networking behavior in the enterprise.

Enterprise-wide Information and Communication Networks

Mastering change requires instantly accessible, enterprise-wide information and communication. This provides the following:

- The information that individual operations require if they are to be reconfigurable
- The rapid internal communications needed to reduce decision time
- The backdrop to entrepreneurship
- The means to keep all the enterprise, and especially decision makers at the periphery, continually informed of the vision, values, mission, and current state

Communication and information networks are today's solution, whether they be intranets, groupware, or any other type of information network. These allow instant communication among individuals throughout the enterprise, the transfer of data files between processes, and storage and widespread information distribution.

The mere presence of these networks does not, however, mean that people will communicate or share information. Whether they do depends on the enterprise's culture of communication and information sharing. We say more about the use of enterprise-wide communication networks and the culture that supports them in Chapter 7. In Chapter 8, we look at the more formal enterprise-wide publishing of information on corporate intranets.

Learning Networks

Mastering change calls for strategies to create and sustain an adaptable work force. This adaptability comes about not only through a personal approach to change, but by having the appropriate work skills to match new demands. Work-force education and training therefore play a key part in creating an adaptable work force. Network learning technologies and agile learning styles are today's answer for enterprise-wide accessibility to learning resources. The potential exists to create electronic, virtual classrooms available 24 hours a day at employees' desks or even homes. This network-mediated approach to learning is described in Chapter 11.

Concurrent Operations Networks

Concurrent operations rely heavily on communication between concurrent processes. When processes were serial, a team's communication could remain largely self-contained. Communication between teams was needed only when inputs were received and outputs handed over. Teams working concurrently, however, demand continuous and intense communication with each other if the work outputs are not to diverge. The scale of this communication must be managed through information and communication protocols that are specially designed to support concurrent operations. Concurrent operations networks require the group communications described in Chapter 7 and the agile, virtual teaming approach described in Chapter 10.

The Bottom Line

Mastering change requires reconfigurable operations and rapid response, undertaken by an adaptable and entrepreneurial work force in an enterprise that makes itself proficient at change. Networking plays an instrumental role in developing this key capability. We have suggested some links between learning, teaming, and agility. In later chapters we'll zoom in on how an organization goes about consciously building these links.

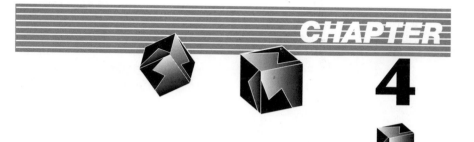

AGILE PRINCIPLES II

The first two agile principles focused on an enterprise's relationships with its customers and environment. The final two address how the enterprise enhances its capability to compete and change by fully exploiting internal assets and reaching out to external assets.

Agile Principle 3: Leveraging Resources

The third principle of agility is leveraging resources. The logic is that in conditions of time and cost competition, an enterprise cannot afford to have any idle or unexploited resources. Of course, every enterprise wants its resources to make an impact. The agile enterprise, however, particularly needs to mobilize all its resources if it is to enrich the customer and master change.

Leveraging resources principally concerns people in the enterprise. People are the most important asset of the agile enterprise, as it is only people who can create agility. Leveraging resources has three top-level strategies: create an entrepreneurial environment, organize for teamwork, and exploit skill and knowledge resources.

Create an Entrepreneurial Environment

The agile enterprise creates an entrepreneurial environment through creating a vision of agility and empowering people and harnessing their commitment to that vision.

A Vision of Entrepreneurship

Creating an entrepreneurial environment first means creating a vision of entrepreneurship for the enterprise. The enterprise may have a favored vision of entrepreneurship. However, agility itself is a powerful entrepreneurial vision. Agile competition and mastery of change capture many of the principles of entrepreneurship. They further identify the personal and enterprise-level strategies though which these can be turned from principles into behavior. Education in agility across the enterprise will greatly assist in forming the vision of entrepreneurship.

Having a vision is one thing; turning that vision into behavior is another. Management needs to act to help people to be committed to the vision and to feel empowered to act on it.

Commitment to the Enterprise

Individuals' commitment to an enterprise is encouraged through the following.

- The entrepreneurial vision needs to be backed up with top-level management commitment and visionary leadership.
- Commitment is increased through open communication. This entails an explicit policy that anyone can communicate with anyone else, regardless of position, department, or function. This sends the message that individuals and their views are valued. By legitimizing upward (junior to senior) communication flows, the enterprise demonstrates its trust in its people and asks for commitment. It also receives valuable input—ideas, criticisms, opportunities—from people close to the customer and to the environment.
- Open communications also create commitment through creating a sense of community. Many enterprises now use network-based discussion forums to reinforce their social fabric. Here communication is not only permitted, it is encouraged, to build a sense of belonging and fellowship.
- Finally, commitment to the enterprise is enhanced if individual compensation is aligned with the enterprise's performance through profit sharing or bonus schemes.

Empowered People

Having a vision and commitment is not enough unless management empowers people in the enterprise to behave in an agile way. Empowering people is the necessary reciprocal action to asking for their commitment. A work force that commits to the entrepreneurial vision needs also to be empowered to act toward that vision.

Empowering people for agility means giving individuals the responsibility to make their own decisions about how they can best be agile. The agile enterprise does this as follows:

- Management is decentralized. Far more decision making is devolved to those who interact with the customer and who engage with the external business environment. Decision makers at the perimeter, though, just like those at the center, need to know the strategic, policy, and practical considerations that should color their decisions. This means that up-to-date strategic information has to be continuously available to them.
- Management encourages risk taking in a supportive, learning environment. Agility means continually dealing with new customer demands and creating new responses to a changing environment. Because so much is always new, far fewer rules and procedures can be specified in advance. Individuals need to be encouraged to take risks—to act on uncertain information in new situations. However, if management reacts critically to a "wrong" outcome, people will soon learn not to risk anything new. Hence, while successes are applauded, so must honest failures. Both are opportunities for learning by asking "What can we learn from this?", rather than "Who do we reward or blame?" This means adopting a learning organization style, using experiences and events to develop systemic individual and enterprise-level knowledge.
- Individuals are made responsible for goals and are given the autonomy to achieve these goals in ways in which they see fit within specified constraints. Management does not control by specifying the precise ways in which goals are to be accomplished.
- Empowering people also means taking notice of them as people, and not as units on an organization chart. Just as enriching the customer requires dealing with customers as individuals, so employees are dealt with as individuals. This can mean, for example, creating flexi-

ble work patterns so that employees can achieve a better work–life balance. It also means recognizing diversity in the workplace. This is not just an ethical nicety. It brings creativity and an understanding of a fragmented marketplace into the enterprise and reinforces the enterprise's commitment to its employees.

Organize for Teamwork

Much work in the agile enterprise is carried out by semiautonomous or self-managing teams. They take the responsibility to achieve a solution for the enterprise or for a customer, rather than to output components to other processes.

Teams and teamwork are exemplary vehicles for agility. We could almost go so far as to say that teams are the basic building block of the truly agile enterprise. In their highly influential book, Katzenbach and Smith[1] describe why teams are such organizationally powerful units for any enterprise. From their description, we can pick out those capabilities of teams that are important for the agile enterprise:

- Because teams are a combination of their members' individual skills, experiences, and judgment, they respond well to multifaceted challenges like innovation, quality, and customer service. All three of these are challenges faced by the agile enterprise in enriching the customer.
- Teams perform better—potentially very significantly better—than a collection of individuals because they are flexible and responsive to changing events and demands. Their ability to respond to change is exactly what is required for mastering change.
- Teams can be more quickly assembled, deployed, refocused, and disbanded than formal groupings such as departments. This is important for agile process reconfigurability.
- Individuals are not exposed in a team. The collective environment means that they are supported when they take risks. We have said that creating an entrepreneurial environment means supporting people in risk taking.

---

1. Jon R. Katzenbach and Douglas K. Smith, *The Wisdom of Teams* (Boston: Harvard Business School Press, 1993).

- Teams are an ideal environment in which to learn and develop. Individuals in teams must learn from each other to integrate their work. Individuals can practice newly learned skills more readily in a team context, because they are not exposed. Indeed, high-performance teams take care of their members' individual learning needs. These are the learning capabilities required for creating an adaptable work force.
- Teams act as a melting pot, playing the role of "change cells." Teams have to work out how to achieve the enterprise's goals in the face of constraints with the skills available to them. They are important vehicles for transitioning to agile behavior.

Katzenbach and Smith say that "Most models of 'the organization of the future' that we have heard about—'networked,' 'clustered,' 'non-hierarchical,' 'horizontal,' and so forth—are premised on teams surpassing individuals as the primary performance unit in the company."[2] This is truer for the agile organization than for any other.

The many advantages of teams are not, however, got without effort and change. Katzenbach and Smith's researches of 47 teams found that the benefits listed above only come from what they term "real teams." These only form under certain conditions. For example, a real team occurs only it takes responsibility for its outcomes, is granted autonomy, and when there is shared accountability and compensation. While an agile enterprise is more able to create these conditions than others, they need to be recognized as strict conditions. Important though teams are to agility, creating them is a challenge.

Exploit Skill and Knowledge Assets

The third strategy for leveraging resources is actively to exploit the skills and knowledge in the enterprise. An agile enterprise cannot afford to maintain assets that are not benefiting the bottom line. Furthermore, changes in customer requirements and the business environment mean that the enterprise cannot rely on the skills and knowledge that it has traditionally found valuable. It must find ways to exploit all that it knows, not just what it has previously recognized that it knows.

Exploiting skill and knowledge assets requires certain capabilities in the enterprise.

2. Katzenbach and Smith, p. 19.

Identified and Valued Skill and Knowledge Assets

For skill and knowledge assets to be exploitable, they have to be identified. This means conducting an inventory to discover where and within whom skill and knowledge reside. This can be approached by concentrating on the following:

1. Core competencies. These are identified by asking this question: "What would your competitors buy from you?"
2. Skills and knowledge required to produce goods and services that customers value.
3. Knowledge about customers, customer relationships, the marketplace, and the wider business environment.
4. Knowledge about critical internal processes (including how to be agile).
5. Other skills and knowledge in the enterprise.

Identifying these leads naturally to valuing them. Valuing can be approached by asking what the impact would be if these assets were not in the enterprise or were in a competitor's enterprise. (There is further discussion of valuing knowledge in Chapter 9.)

Agility says something additional to a typical inventory of skills and knowledge. In the agile world, the importance of some identifiable skill or knowledge may change. What always remains valuable, however, is knowing how that skill or knowledge was created. In the ever-changing agile world, it is the processes that create skill and knowledge that are important.

Skills and Knowledge Accessible Everywhere, Anytime

Once skills and knowledge have been identified, there must be means to connect them to people in the enterprise who may need them. This means creating the systems to allow enterprise-wide access to this knowledge. For skills, it means creating directories of who has what skills and then making it easy for people who need particular skills to connect to people who have them.

Skill and Knowledge Creation and Capture

An inventory of skills and knowledge cannot afford only to be retrospective. It must be forward looking, asking questions about how skill and knowledge will be created and captured in future.

Skill and Knowledge Development

The preceding process will have identified the key skills and knowledge in the enterprise. It will also have identified gaps between the skill and knowledge required to perform critical processes and those present in the enterprise. Hence an important aspect of exploiting skills and knowledge is creating or accelerating systems that allow people to acquire and develop skills and knowledge. This means education, training, and coaching systems.

Lean Core with Contingent Resources

Exploiting skill and knowledge assets also means knowing which assets the enterprise should not directly own. Outsourcing low-value skills and knowledge should be considered. This leaves a leaner core, which can call on outsourced skills and knowledge when required. Such a leaner core is more agile, because it holds less overhead. Outsourced skills and knowledge remain accessible, however, because they are retained in agile partnering and supply relationships, as discussed later.

The Networking Dimension

Leveraging resources depends heavily in today's enterprise on its networking capabilities.

Open Communications

While a key aspect of open communications is policy and practice, networks themselves are significant enablers. Communication networks let people throughout the enterprise communicate with each other. They vastly increase the number of people with whom one can communicate easily—from the few people one sees at one's workplace to hundreds and possibly thousands throughout the enterprise. We describe these communication networks in Chapter 7.

Community Building

Enterprise-wide discussion forums, or group conferences, are a powerful means of building a sense of community. People from all parts of the enterprise can communicate in self-forming interest groups. They can express themselves to others and be exposed to a diversity of other views. These conferences can create what approaches a clublike atmosphere. They prevent fragmentation and feelings of remoteness from the enterprise and increase the sense of belonging and fellowship with others.

Chapter 7 presents specific data on how communication networks increase commitment.

Information Circulation

We discussed earlier, in the context of mastering change, the need for the agile enterprise to decentralize decision making. To support their decision making, people at the periphery need constant, up-to-date information about the enterprise—its values, mission, strategies, news, and current threats and opportunities. The most efficient answer to spreading information widely is information networks. We talk about the communication aspects of information circulation in Chapter 7 and the more formal informational aspects, in the context of intranet publishing, in Chapter 8.

Virtual Team Networks

Teams are highly important and effective vehicles for agility, and the conditions that allow real teams to form are consistent with those of an agile enterprise. Teams and agility go hand in hand. But teams do not have to be restricted to those people who happen to work in the same location nor to those who can be cajoled to travel to a team hub. Information and communication networks very efficiently support virtual teams. These are teams whose members are distributed geographically and often organizationally. They maintain intense communication with each other using a variety of networking tools: email and audio-, video-, and group-conferencing. Virtual team networks allow the agile enterprise to use the power of teams regardless of where team members happen to be. We explore virtual and agile teams in detail in Chapter 10.

Knowledge Management

Exploiting skill and knowledge is the agile enterprise's prescription for making its assets—and especially its people assets—benefit the enterprise. In the period since this aspect of agility was first highlighted, this idea has become one of the fastest-growing business topics—under the title "knowledge management." Now, hundreds of articles and conference papers are devoted to knowledge management strategies. In each case, knowledge management takes place in a networked environment. Networks are recruited to capture knowledge and to store and spread knowledge and maps of knowledge. They are the means to get knowledge from people who have it to people who need it, at the right time. Knowledge management in the agile, networked enterprise is the subject of Chapter 9.

The Bottom Line

Leveraging resources means leveraging people's energy and commitment in an entrepreneurial environment and taking stock of and mobilizing all the enterprise's valued skills and knowledge. Networks play a central role—greatly increasing the ease of making connections with people, information, and knowledge throughout the enterprise.

Agile Principle 4: Cooperating to Compete

The final principle of agility is cooperating to compete. The logic of this principle is that the agile enterprise cannot go it alone. Just as leveraging resources is needed to mobilize the enterprise's internal assets for agility, cooperating to compete is about reaching out to external assets. Having recourse to external assets is important for several reasons:

1. Agility requires a range of unpredictable new responses. There will be times when a needed capability does not exist in-house or cannot feasibly be developed in-house. It needs to be got—ready to run—from outside.

2. Agile enterprises share the cost of R&D for a greater diversity of products with other enterprises.

3. Agile enterprises get products to market quicker through cooperating with partners and suppliers that provide contributory solutions.

4. Agile enterprises need to cooperate with other enterprises to enter into niche markets and new worldwide marketplaces.

5. Cooperating with other suppliers allows an agile enterprise to create solutions for the end customer.

6. Outsourced skills and knowledge remain available through close cooperative relationships.

The agile enterprise actively seeks the right cooperative relationships, rather than shying away from them. It is confident in cooperating because it is confident that it has prepared itself fully. Cooperation becomes regarded as a competency of the enterprise, rather than something fearful and highly risky. There are a number of strategies for reliably and effectively cooperating with other enterprises. We are generically calling these *partnering* strategies.

Build Proficiency in Partnering

The first strategy for cooperating to compete is to build proficiency in partnering. Note that this is directed at proficiency in *partnering*—with anyone and for any reason—and not for dealing with any particular *partner.* Recall that, similarly, part of mastering change was building proficiency *to change,* not ability to make *a change.* This means a number of preparatory activities.

Pro Forma Business Case for Partnering

The agile enterprise builds a generic, pro forma business case for partnering. This is essentially educational. It shows how to create metrics for the value of building, buying, or partnering to develop solutions. It shows how to assess the value of the relationship created, the opportunity to integrate a value chain, the value of the resources obtained, and the value of time to market. It shows how to weigh these advantages against considerations of finance, time scale and program, legality and risk.

Inventory of Intellectual Property

Every enterprise is rightly concerned about protecting its commercial secrets. This can lead to anxious, uncomfortable negotiations with potential partners and failure to find rewarding relationships.

The agile enterprise realizes that what it can and cannot share becomes a hot issue when partnerships are being struck. It also realizes that intellectual property sharing is a black hole that sucks in time, effort, emotion, and potential good business. It therefore sets out to assess and codify its intellectual property and draw up rules about how it can and cannot be shared.

Assessing intellectual property is very similar to the process described earlier for identifying and valuing skill and knowledge assets. Indeed, the same framework and questions can be asked. The point made earlier in that context, however, needs to be made again. In the ever-changing agile world, the processes that create intellectual property are as or more important than an item of intellectual property itself. In assessing intellectual property, the enterprise should explicitly consider whether it can share the processes that generate its intellectual property.

We say more about this in Chapter 9. The result will be an inventory of the enterprise's intellectual property, together with rules for the conditions under which it can be shared under what disclosure restrictions. With this inventory in their pockets, managers negotiating a partnership will be relieved of a major source of worry.

Code for Forming and Dissolving Partnerships

Agile partnerships form and dissolve. A partnering relationship does not persist longer than the business case that requires it. And new partnerships are formed rapidly, even with previous partners in new contexts. The amount of partnering that the agile enterprise will be involved in requires it to have a preformed code for forming and dissolving partnerships. This will include a pro forma legal instrument. In *Cooperate to Compete*,[3] Preiss and colleagues specifically advise that such a legal instrument should not seek to anticipate every possible problem or dispute. It is more important that it sets out the processes by which a dispute can be solved.

Cultural Literacy

Partnering will not always be with enterprises who share the same culture. It may be necessary to partner with an enterprise with a very different organizational culture or, in working worldwide, to partner with an enterprise based in a different national culture. Culture is a system of fundamental, taken-for-granted assumptions about the way the world is. Cultures differ in the way that they view hierarchy, time, work, information, communication, and conflict, among others. Cultural differences can lead to profound misunderstandings between partners. Consequently, the agile enterprise needs to become culturally literate. This means being able to articulate its own culture and to understand the business implications of different organizational and national cultures.

Profiles of Potential Partners

An agile enterprise can move quickly into a partnering relationship to meet urgent customer-driven demands if it has already created a set of profiles of potential partners. Such a profile can include the following items:

- Core competencies we are particularly interested in
- Other valuable skills and knowledge
- Their likely interest in our intellectual property
- Our intellectual property that we cannot share with them
- Their proficiency at enriching the customer
- Their proficiency at mastering change
- Their proficiency at leveraging resources

---

3. Kenneth Preiss, Steven L. Goldman, and Roger N. Nagel, *Cooperate to Compete* (New York: Van Nostrand Reinhold, 1996), pp. 166–7.

- Their proficiency at partnering, including record of past and present partners
- Organizational and national culture and implications

Make Partnering a Strategy of Choice

Having built its proficiency in partnering, the agile enterprise needs to engage everyone in seeing partnering as an opportunity. Much of the threat of partnering will have been removed through developing the material described. Stakeholders throughout the enterprise now need to see partnering as a strategy of choice and not of last resort.

The stakeholders to whom a vision of partnering needs to be explained and iterated are likely to include the following:

- Senior management, and especially owner-founders who may be more reluctant that others to accept the need for partnering
- Middle management, who need to see partnering as a way to profit and success, and not as a lessening of influence
- The work force, who need likewise to see partnering as a means of sustaining the enterprise and not of reducing staff
- Key customers, who need to see the added potential of a supplier who has access to more resources to better meet their requirements; they also need to be reassured that any proprietary information already shared will not leak to partners
- Possibly, the press and public, in the case of a significant instance of partnering

Be a Valued Partner

It takes two (or more) to partner. Not only has the agile enterprise to build proficiency in partnering, but it has also to be an attractive, valued partner. Much of its attraction will come from its core competencies and skills, its agility, and its customers and markets. However, if the enterprise has built proficiency in partnering, this proficiency itself will be valued. Intending partners will find it comfortable to negotiate with an enterprise that shows confidence and skills in partnering. Moreover, the enterprise may find that it has a negotiating strength because it has already thought through its partnering strategies.

However, proficiency in partnering is not all that is needed to be a valued partner. Additionally, the enterprise needs to be known for its trustworthiness. It must have a reputation for keeping its word, nonpredatory behavior, respect for the rights of its partners—whether or not enshrined in a legal document—and a willingness to share risk. In some contexts, it may need explicitly to confirm its adherence to technical, quality, social, and cultural standards.

Operate a Virtual Organization

So far we have discussed the preparatory strategies for cooperating to compete. These are the strategies that lead up to forming a partnership. The remaining strategy is that of successfully operating with one or more partners. The form of this operation is a virtual organization. It is an organization because it has a purpose, structure, and members and undertakes some activity. It is virtual because it exists between and among two or more partners.

We therefore describe next how partner enterprises need to operate with the virtual organization that they have formed. There are of course a large number of issues to do with the way in which the virtual organization itself operates. We deal with these in Chapter 14 in the context of agile networked alliances. For the time being, however, we deal only with the key issues that a partner enterprise needs to recognize.

As will be seen in the following, much of what is known about teams and teaming[4] is in principle applicable to virtual organizations. It is also often directly applicable, since the embodiment of a virtual organization is often itself a team.

A Clear and Relevant Purpose with Measurable Goals

The virtual organization will have a purpose for existence. This purpose needs to be clear, and progress toward it must be measured by clear performance goals. Its purpose must also be obviously consistent with the partners' goals. If its purpose is all these, the virtual organization will form and operate readily and be supported by its partners. If the purpose is unclear or progress is not measured, partners will start to question their involvement.

---

4. Our basic reference on teams and teaming is Katzenbach and Smith, *The Wisdom of Teams.*

To those who say that this is motherhood, we say that we have seen numerous alliances, "cooperative networks," and "joint task forces" fail because partners were lazy in defining purpose.

Capability-based Membership

A virtual organization will value people for their capabilities and skills. Position and authority in their home enterprise will usually count for little. In situations where people experience removal of position and authority, partners need to recognize that this can be unsettling and act or counsel accordingly.

Partners must be prepared to let the virtual organization have considerable say in who is selected to staff it. People cannot be simply assigned according to what is convenient to a partner. The virtual organization, if it is not already legally constituted as such, needs to be regarded as a separate enterprise that is bidding for staff.

Autonomy Granted

Partners must recognize that its people in a virtual organization have two obligations. There are obligations to itself and obligations to the new virtual organization. A partner may expect its people to feel the former more strongly than the latter. On that basis it may be seductive for a partner to meddle. It may want to set its people covert tasks and targets. It may want silently to take them off for other jobs or replace them at short notice. This creates an impossible situation for the people involved and is anyway untrustworthy. It also spells doom for the virtual organization itself.

Every partner must give its people—and the whole virtual organization—autonomy. Autonomy means defining goals and the structure and working methods that fulfill these goals. If a partner has concerns or issues about such autonomy, they need to be openly addressed to the management of the virtual organization. Again, the virtual organization should be regarded as an autonomous enterprise, subject to normal interenterprise dealings.

Defined Lifetime

The purpose of many virtual organizations is long term, for example, an agreement to form a joint venture company or to act together as suppliers. Other purposes will be more short term, typically to undertake a task or project. Partners need to recognize that it is only that purpose that holds the virtual organization together in a business sense. If the purpose is short term, so is the virtual organization. Hence, unlike most enterprises and like most teams, a virtual enterprise has a defined lifetime. This lifetime needs to be explicit to the virtual organization and part of its operating plan. It also means that the virtual organization is a reasonably low risk affair. If things are not exactly to a partner's satisfaction, then they will at least be short.

The Networking Dimension

Networked Virtual Organizations
In our discussion of virtual organizations, we made no assumptions about their physical form. They might be collocated or dispersed and communicate face to face, by post, or by electronic means. We did not make any assumptions earlier because they were not relevant to our discussion. However, it is in reality almost impossible to talk about virtual organizations today without assuming that they are distributed and networked.

Almost without exception, today's virtual organizations are not only composed of people from different enterprises; they are composed of people who work from different locations and who communicate and conduct their work over a network. They therefore represent a major shift in the way that work is done and managed. We talk much more about the networked virtual organization in the context of more general agile networked alliances in Chapter 14. For now, we simply note that virtual organization is today synonymous with network.

The Bottom Line

Cooperating to compete means becoming proficient in partnering, actively seeking partners, and being an attractive partner. Once a partnership has formed, the enterprise has to give it purpose and autonomy. Networks are today's de facto workplace for the virtual organization that these partnerships create.

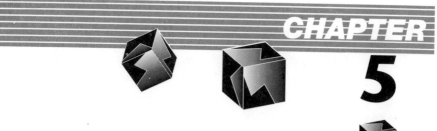

AGILITY CHANGE DOMAINS

In this final chapter dealing with agility, we'll look at some ways enterprises can measure just how agile they are. We must keep in mind the Duchess of Windsor's advice;[1] there's no ultimate quantitative goal for agility: no six-sigma or perfect ten. Change does not stop, so agility, and the processes for being agile, are themselves ongoing. But to enable enterprises to determine where they are on the agility spectrum, a robust set of formal instruments has been developed and is being implemented by The Agility Forum. These instruments contain analytical tools, metrics, and best agile practices. They are based on the idea of *change proficiency domains*: eight well-defined categories of agile capability. Each category addresses specific agility goals, strategies, processes, and metrics. Each provides a way of measuring performance in the areas of agility that an enterprise considers are important to the competitive challenges it faces.

For example, a supplier of fabrics to the automotive and furniture industries, we'll call it Company Y, realizes that it is turning away a lot of work because of capacity limitations, both low and high end.

---

1. "You can't be too rich or too thin," on which basis we said in Chapter 1 that "You cannot be agile enough."

- At the low end, it cannot adapt to service the needs of niche customers. This is because it costs too much to switch a large production line to produce just a few thousand yards of a specialty product. But Company Y's customers are investing increasingly in niche products that need small-volume runs. And more flexible competitors are getting a growing share of Company Y's customer base.
- At the high end of the spectrum, Company Y has been refusing sudden orders for large amounts of product because of lack of production capacity. Again, the result is lost opportunity and possibly lost customers.

To address its problems, Company Y looks into the *capacity* change proficiency domain. Here can be found clues to the capabilities and practices that help companies like Company Y to attain greater flexibility. Using tools developed by The Agility Forum, Company Y finds high-leverage points for investment and proceeds to develop agility in precisely the areas it needs to better respond to customers demands.

Keep in mind that what is measured is not how much product is sold or the efficiency of the fabric manufacturing process. What is measured is the *capability of the organization to respond to change in demand.* That is, if in the past Company Y turned away 80% of customer requests that required significant deviation from its standard production parameters, then it would have a flexibility rating of 20%. If it wanted to achieve a rating of 80%, it would need to address the areas of the capacity change domain that enable flexibility. In the case of Company Y, this could involve two investments:

1. For small batches, set up a line that uses advanced, automated processes to enable fast turn around. Train people to think niche in its marketing, sales, and production departments. Create pricing algorithms that reflect the customer's valuing time more than commodity volumes. In terms of agile principles, learn to manage change and deliver customer solutions.

2. For very large batches, ensure that alliances are in place with agile partners who can pick up capacity. From their perspective, Company Y may be offering them niche work that they are capable of taking up. In other words, cooperate to compete.

Change proficiency domains are referred to often in agility literature, the leading expert being Rick Dove of The Agility Forum and Paradigm Shift International.[2] Dove has used change domains as a tool to look at agility from a variety of perspectives. Here we'll discuss change proficiency domains in just enough detail to provide a basis for their extension into agile networking.

The Change Proficiency Domains

There are eight change proficiency domains:

1. Creation
2. Capacity
3. Capability
4. Reconfiguration
5. Migration
6. Performance
7. Improvement
8. Recovery

We'll define each one briefly:

Creation

This covers the creation or deletion of organizational initiatives: projects, product, process, or technology development. That is, knowing when to start and knowing when to stop. Not so easy as it seems. At one time the present authors worked for a computer manufacturer whose ability to start new projects was legendary and whose current products list ranged in the tens of thousands. However, many new projects led up blind alleys, consumed resources needed elsewhere, or produced products that no one wanted. And many of the "available products" had long gathered cobwebs. As the rate of change in market demands increased, the lack of focus on new ventures and inability to stop efforts once they got underway severely affected the company's performance.

2. In this discussion we draw primarily on Rick Dove's article "Agile Supply Chain Management," *Automotive Production*, April 1996.

Capacity

We've already had a look at this: the flexibility to handle increases or decreases in demand. A classic example of the value of addressing the capacity domain comes from Dow Corning Corporation. When faced with a significant increase in demand for one of its products, Dow Corning found it did not have the piping capacity to meet the customer's demand.[3] In analyzing the problem, they discovered that they had made a decision to use smaller pipe when building the facility—saving a few thousand dollars. However, the impact of not having the capacity was in the hundreds of thousands of dollars. Future capacity decisions, using proficiency analysis, ensured that they did not again save pennies to lose dollars!

Capability

Often (usually, these days) an enterprise needs to augment its internal capabilities—knowledge, skills, technology—in order to take advantage of an opportunity. This is the agility principle of cooperating to compete. Agile performance here is the speed with which the enterprise can find a partner to provide that capability. This involves being prepared for just such a situation and having the processes in place to find, qualify, and integrate that partner's competency into the culture and work flow.

Reconfiguration

Examples of excellence in this domain, which refers explicitly to mastering change, often involve the rapid reconfiguration of fixtures on a shop floor, partitions in an open office, or other physical artifacts. But this applies equally to reconfiguring teams as missions and tasks change. Enterprises that have a sound understanding of their people's competencies, not just their job titles, usually do better in this category.

Migration

Obvious examples of migration proficiency exist in people adopting new technology systems. But migration takes many forms, some strategic. For example, an energy company decides to migrate its culture from largely self-contained, "stovepiped" divisions to a corporate knowledge-sharing

---

3. The example of Dow Corning Corporation is discussed, along with other examples of change proficiency domains, in The Agility Forum's videotape "Change Domains" (Bethlehem, PA: The Agility Forum, 1995).

community through a massive "best practices" initiative. Their proficiency in the migration domain will determine how effectively and economically they can make this happen.

Performance

Performance speaks primarily to issues of quality. Evidence of proficiency here would include effective processes for incorporating changes to specifications (ECOs), integrating the "voice of the customer" into new product and service designs, and the ability to measure and improve quality in a systemic way. There's nothing new about quality as a first-order consideration for all enterprises, from component manufacturers, to transportation services, to educational institutions. Agility focuses on sustaining and improving quality in the face of change.

Improvement

An enterprise's core competencies comprise the knowledge, skill, technologies, and even culture that competitors envy. In the current environment of continually escalating market demands, intensifying competition, and evolving technology, these core competencies cannot stagnate but must constantly improve. An example of agility in this domain would be an enterprise's systemic learning infrastructure. These are the processes that provide continuous, just-in-time, just-in-place development of competencies, as will be discussed in Chapter 11.

Recovery

This final change domain involves being prepared for problems such as supplier failure, departure of key personnel, layoffs, or mergers: expecting the unexpected. Just as the modern telephone system uses dynamic switching to get around point failures in the network, enterprises must have processes in place to recover from unpredictable show-stopping events.

Assessing Change Proficiency

Each domain described above defines an area of agile performance that can be analyzed, measured, and improved. Rick Dove defines four operative elements of change domains:

1. *Change proficiency:* the competency in which the adaptation or change occurs

2. *Change proficiency metric:* the performance item that is measured to provide a value for comparison (e.g., time, cost, robustness, scope)

3. *Change proficiency issue:* the activity to which the metric will be applied

4. *Change proficiency measure:* units of the metric

To illustrate these basic elements, we'll look again at the example we used in defining the creation domain (or, more specifically, creation or deletion).

If, at the time we were working for the computer manufacturer, we had known about agility, we might have noted the strategic importance of improving the company's *change proficiency* in the *creation domain.* Specifically, we would have investigated the *change proficiency issue* of stopping "loser" projects. We'd use the *change proficiency metrics* of time and cost, represented in the *change proficiency measures* of numbers of days and thousands of dollars.

A change proficiency analysis done in 1990 might have looked like that shown in Table 5–1. This change proficiency analysis shows clearly the gap between present nonagile capabilities and the level of agility to be reached one year later. Of course, at this point a decision to design "close-down" processes would need to be made, along with investment, scheduling, and all the other operational commitments required to make a reality out of a laudable goal.

Table 5–1 Change Proficiency Analysis for Creation or Deletion.

Change Domain	Creation or deletion
Change Proficiency Issue	Stopping an existing project
Metric	Time and cost
Measure	Days or $ millions
Change Proficiency	
June 1990 (as-is state)	420/1,700 (estimated)
June 1991 (to be target)	100/400

Change domains bring a focus to the wide sweep of agility that is essential to providing sound business rationale for investing in agile capabilities. As a general approach, it is recommended that enterprises take an *and* rather than an *or* approach to addressing agility. They should spend time to determine what the highest leveraged agility domains are and then evenly invest in developing them. The balanced agility that results will provide better performance than drilling down in one area at the expense of other equally important areas.

We will return to the discussion of change domains in Chapter 6, this time in the context of the agile *networking* change domains that provide high-leveraged points for developing agility.

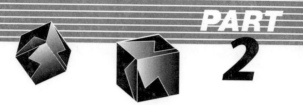

Agile Networking
Capabilities

Part 2 explores an enterprise's agile capabilities, establishing the foundation for the next part which deals with agile operations.

Here we bring networking and agility together, addressing communication, information, and knowledge, the "coins of the realm" of agility. We begin by focusing on "switching," that aspect of networking that directly addresses change, and therefore agility.

While we touch on the key points of networking, the purpose here is not to duplicate extensive work already done, but to show the core role of networking in achieving agility.

Next we devote individual chapters to group communication and to intranet publication. The point here is to highlight the differences between these capabilities: publication does not effect group communication, conventional belief notwithstanding. These modes of sharing information are certainly facilitated by networks, but in different ways, to different purposes.

Finally, we discuss knowledge management. Again, often confused with publication of information or tracking of communications. In agile work knowledge has no intrinsic value. Its worth to the enterprise lies in its being identifiable, accessible and capable of being applied quickly in concert with other knowledge.

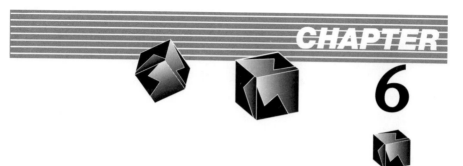

NETWORKING
AND AGILITY

Treat interchanges as primary and transportation lines as secondary. Create incentives so that all the different modes of public transportation . . . plan their lines to connect the interchanges, with the hope that gradually many different lines, of many different types, will meet at every interchange.

—Christopher Alexander, et al.[1]

Agility, then, is about an enterprise's systemic capabilities to respond to and anticipate change: to be ready for the realities of today's business environment. We propose that a strategic commitment to networking can provide a rapid path to achieving agility in areas vital to competitive success.

The Networking Model

First, let's talk briefly about networking as an organizational concept. As we pointed out earlier, networking is not a new idea, but has become increasingly sophisticated with the understanding of virtual relationships and teaming processes.

1. Christopher Alexander, Sara Ishikawa, and Murray Silverstein, "The Web of Public Transportation," in *A Pattern Language: Towns, Buildings, Construction*, ed. Alexander, Ishikawa, and Silverstein (New York: Oxford University Press, 1977), p. 94.

Links, Nodes, and Purpose

The basic model of networking is that it has three components. These are (1) peer level relationships (*links*), between (2) people, objects, or systems (*nodes*), created to accomplish (3) a specific *purpose*. Purpose can range from the relatively casual desire of a group of professionals to keep in touch, to a stronger need to link documents on the World Wide Web, to the very powerful purpose that binds a team working on a new product or service.[2]

People, Processes, and Technology

Organizational networking can be approached from a variety of perspectives. One traditional way is through the lenses of people, processes, and technologies.

- People networking is essential to the concept of teams. Networking means communicating, and teams do their work largely through communication.
- Equally important are networking processes: the designed use of communications media and applications to facilitate the accomplishment of work. In Chapter 10 we'll look at some very sophisticated networking processes that enable global teams to sustain complex programs such as sales support, just-in-time learning, and best practices knowledge-based access.
- The technology of networking evolves on a daily basis, but essentially involves the media that carry messages and the applications that provide access to the media, for example, local-area networks (LANs), wide-area networks (WANs), municipal-area networks (MANs), long lines, satellites, phones, modems, and, really, PCs. In the mainstream economic world of today, the communications infrastructure is ubiquitous: the issue is not whether points are connected, but why, when, and how they are connected.

---

2. We are happy to acknowledge long-time colleagues Jessica Lipnack and Jeffrey Stamps as the originators of the purpose, teams, and links model. It's most recently expressed in their book *Virtual Teams: Reaching Across Space, Time and Organizations with Technology* (New York: John Wiley & Sons, Inc., 1997).

The Networking Matrix

Orthogonal to the perspectives of people, process, and technology are the three components of any network system: purpose, nodes, and links.

1. In organizational networking, we assume that a purpose exists. This purpose defines the need for particular nodes to be connected by specific kinds of links. For example, a distributed team engaged in creating a new consumer product has as its purpose to deliver the product.

2. The nodes involved would be the team participants, the points of work and deliverables in the process, and the communications devices and applications.

3. Links for the people nodes include team bonding elements like trust, understanding of each other's work expectations, and commitment to sharing information and knowledge. Technology links include whatever media provide the connectivity and bandwidth required; whether it be in-state phone and fax or global satellite video. Process links might involve information and time flow.

We can look at this instance of a networking situation as a matrix, as shown in Figure 6–1.

Situation: Global team develops a product specification			
	People	Process	Technology
Nodes	Participants in UK, Norway, US	Products Information Objects (documents)	PCs, e-mail, shared CAD, leased video conferencing equipment
Links	Relationships, Trust, Knowledge Sharing, Expectations	Time, Information and Knowledge Flow	Media: – LANs – WANs – etc.
Purpose	Drawn together to develop specification	Goals, tasks, timescales	Configuration of network

Figure 6–1 Networking System Matrix: Global team develops a specification.

Networking then, in the sense that we use it here, is a structured work model that supports distributed teams using telecommunications and information technologies to accomplish information and knowledge-based work. Now we'll look at networking in the context of agility.

Agile Networking

Agile networking denotes the use of networking specifically to address the principles of agility. In particular, we argue that networking proficiency is a highly effective way for an organization to meet the challenges of change in all aspects of the work environment. Staying within the networking metaphor, while networking addresses a general work paradigm, agile networking focuses on networking as a response to change.

In some ways, agile networking brings in the notion of *switching*. Nodes and links adapt in response to or anticipation of changes in purpose; new kinds of links enable formulation of new purposes, and so on.

Agile networking basically involves being able to respond to a change in purpose, intent, or task with appropriate shifts in nodes or links.[3] The *speed, efficiency,* and *effectiveness* with which these switches are made is a measure of the organization's agility. In later chapters we'll focus on this switching capability as instrumental to agility by looking at specific organizational activities such as group communications, on-line publishing, managing knowledge, and continuous learning. Here we'll illustrate possible permutations with some general examples.

Change in Purpose Drives Change in Nodes

- Most new products, programs, or products involve new people (nodes) in the work. Sometimes these are nodes within the enterprise.
- But nodes can also be outside the enterprise; the essence of the virtual alliance as we discuss it in Chapter 14. A new opportunity appears and the lead organization creates alliances with the competencies—the nodes—required to provide a solution. The organization is not limited to "doing what it does," but can team with other nodes to a more sophisticated purpose. For example, a telecom company

---

3. We know this oversimplifies some pretty complex, multivariate events: both links and nodes may change in response to a change in purpose. But for clarity we'll stay at the one-on-one level.

decides that there is a rich market for "mobile sales force support" not limited to "selling minutes on the network." The company allies with technology partners to produce a solution involving hardware, software, and telecom services.

Change in Purpose Drives Change in Links

- A new product team involves new links between members. Previously, these were nonexistent or just familial links of belonging to the same enterprise. Now they are intense, network-enabled communication links.
- In another context, California State University restates its purpose as meeting the needs of California's learning stakeholders (see Chapter 16), rather than continuously expanding campus-based learning. It augments the traditional link to the learner—the classroom—with satellite and Internet links to help to meet this new purpose.

Change in Links Drives Change in Purpose

- Any number of new Internet service-based enterprises have mushroomed in recent years. The new linking mechanism has opened up new profitable purposes for businesses.
- For example, many IT companies have now replaced phone links for software support with the Internet. They then start using this same channel to deliver software and news services.

Change in Links Drives Change in Nodes

- New Internet services enterprises reach new customers (nodes) anywhere in the world.
- For example, the growing availability of satellite delivery channels and Internet opens up a new customer base for the virtual universities: the professional at his or her workplace.
- Ubiquitous communication means that specialist resources can be brought into a project from anywhere in the world at anytime.

Change in Nodes Drives Change in Purpose

- New database servers can alter the purpose of an agile enterprise. Mailing lists become a product, not just a means of marketing.
- A company takes over another; thus acquiring new nodes. The new company changes its purpose to exploit the skills of its newly added people.

Change in Nodes Drives Change in Links

- Stakeholders change; facilities change; technology changes. Agility involves changes to links to turn this change to advantage. We see this daily as worldwide commerce recognizes the growing Internet literacy of the consumer. Almost overnight, advertising has seized the Internet as a marketing channel; "www.you-name-it.com" is now more common than the physical address of the advertiser.
- The agile enterprise's new product team recognizes that it needs external resources. Adopting the agile principle of cooperating to compete, it creates an alliance with a specialist engineering firm an ocean away and maintains close and constant communication with it through the Internet.

Having established networking at a high level as an enabler of agility, we can now look at some specific areas of agility where networking provides high leverage. First, we'll go back to the concept of change proficiency domains discussed in Chapter 5.

Agile Networking Change Domains

We remember from Chapter 5 the set of eight change domains that provide entry points for measuring agility:

1. Creation
2. Capacity
3. Capability
4. Reconfiguration
5. Migration

6. Performance

7. Improvement

8. Recovery

Extending the spirit, if not the letter of these domains into the agile networking arena, we can define indicators of agile networking. Looking at an enterprise's networking capabilities in these areas will provide both a measure of *current effectiveness* in using networking to thrive amid change and indications of where *investment* in networking can have the highest payback. In effect, we have an *agile networking scorecard*, as shown in Figure 6–2. Each cell in the matrix shown in Figure 6–2 can be populated with the appropriate networking capability (nodes and links) suited to the purpose. And this networking capability will in turn address the people, process and technology aspects of the particular domain.

Ways of actually scoring this matrix will be discussed in Chapter 13 in the context of agile management.

Later chapters in Parts 2 and 3 address each of the networking—now agile networking—capabilities noted in the matrix: Agile Group Communications, Agile Intranet Publishing, Agile Knowledge Management, Agile Learning Services, Agile Teaming, and Agile Management.

Networking Capability

Agility Change Domain	Group Communication	Intranet Publishing	Knowledge Management	Learning Services	Teaming	Management
Creation						
Capacity						
Capability						
Reconfiguration						
Migration						
Performance						
Improvement						
Recovery						

Figure 6–2 The agile networking scorecard.

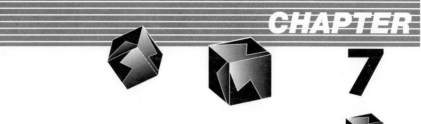

AGILE GROUP COMMUNICATION

This chapter looks at group communication strategies, patterns, and behavior in the agile enterprise. We explore, in agile terms, the situation in which a group of people takes part in an electronically mediated discussion or when enterprise-wide discussion forums are created.

We only touch on email briefly in this chapter. The message here is that group communication is what agility needs, not individual to individual communication.

Neither is this chapter about publishing information, which is essentially about broadcasting prepared information—today on intranet web pages. The essence of information publishing is very different from that of people communicating together. Information publishing has its own value and implications for the agile enterprise, and we discuss these in Chapter 8.

We are, therefore, using communication in its old-fashioned sense of people in dialogue and discussion with each other. Our focus is how this is done in groups, for the purposes of agility, using today's networking tools.

Relevance to Agility

Here we describe the reasons why group communication is important to the agile enterprise. We pull together the aspects of the agile networking dimension discussed in Part 1 that are relevant to group communication.

For mastering change, we saw that the agile enterprise requires instantly accessible, enterprise-wide information and communication. We said that this provided the following:

- The information that individual operations require if they are to be reconfigurable
- Rapid internal communications to reduce decision time
- The means to keep everyone in the enterprise continually informed of the vision, values, mission, and current state of the enterprise

We also saw that leveraging resources required a number of agile network capabilities:

- One requirement for exploiting skill and knowledge assets was to create a knowledge network within the organization.
- We also saw that part of empowering people was creating a sense of community and belonging to the enterprise.
- Another part of empowering people was open communication within the enterprise.
- We finally saw, in the context of leveraging resources, the same requirement as we had seen for mastering change, which is to keep everyone in the enterprise continually informed.

Hence agility gives us the following requirements for communication within the enterprise:

- Enterprise-wide communication
- Knowledge networking
- The means to keep everyone informed of what is going on—at the enterprise, departmental, and group or team level
- Communication to build commitment
- Open communication

We'll discuss each of these communication processes in more detail later in this chapter. Next however, we begin explaining why we see group communication as more agile than individual-to-individual, email communication.

Why Is Group Communication Agile?

A Note about Email

We're not saying throw out your email systems if you want to be agile. Email is a widespread, easily understood, readily adopted communications medium. Even when group communications are available, email is vital for private, person-to-person messages. It's of value when there is no group to communicate with.

Neither is email an inferior communication medium. Our point is that for the agile enterprise it's group communication that provides the agile spin. Hence what we do here is to raise the profile of group communication to make our readers fully aware of its value to agility.

We also guess that our readers already use email or are familiar enough with it not to want more detail about it here. But our readers may not have much experience with group communication systems or their applications.

Much of the reason that group communication in networks is more agile than person-to-person communication has to do with the features and capabilities of what we call group conferencing tools. So we will first review the properties of group conferencing tools.

Group Conferencing Tools

We are using the term *group conferencing* to refer to group exchange of principally text messages. This used to be called computer conferencing, but now has various names: computer conferencing, text conferencing, data conferencing, bulletin boards, groupware, intranet discussion bases, or intranet newsgroups. The products that provide group conferencing today typically include the words notes, team, forum, talk, board, or share in their names, but not all do.

Group conferencing, under the name of computer conferencing, was invented in the late 1970s. In the 1990s, Internet newsgroups are a public embodiment of group conferencing and intranet newsgroups the in-house embodiment. Web-compatible intranet discussion systems are now emerging, combining the core features of 1970s computer conferencing with 1990s web accessibility and platform independence.

All real group conferencing tools share a common set of properties:

- They allow people in a group to exchange written messages using a computer connected to a network.
- People do not have to be located together to use group conferencing. Participants in a group conference are usually widely dispersed across cities, countries, or continents.
- Everything that everyone in the group writes is readable by everyone else in the group.
- A computer stores everything that everyone writes. So people can read the conference record and write new messages whenever it is convenient to them. People don't have to be at their computers at the same time to take part in a group conference.
- There is always an index of past messages of some form available to each user. Sometimes the index is only chronological. More usually, however, messages are organized by subject matter into what are known as threads or topics.

Hence the essence of group conferencing is indexed written messages exchanged among a group through communication that is place independent and time independent.

Using a Group Conference to Support Project Communications

Here's an illustration of how a group conference can be used to support a small project. We're including this example because it's a real-life example of the use of group conferencing to support a project. Also, the project itself had many agile hallmarks. It involved a small number of people charged to do something new very quickly with minimum overhead and to be close to the customer while doing so. It's not unlike a number of projects that are common in agile enterprises today.

Apart from having access group conferencing technology, there's no insurmountable reason why any enterprise cannot run fast-track concurrent projects like this. So, as we describe this project, consider if a similar project could run in your enterprise—and if not, why not.

Two of us were involved in this group conference in 1990. We were in a group creating a prototype information product for an international computer systems and services company. Our group had 10 members at six separate locations in Ireland, England, Germany, and the United States.

For most of the group, this prototype development was a part-time activity. The group conference was created on the company's in-house network and was private (that is, had a controlled membership). It took about half an hour to create the conference itself.

Using this conference, over a period of roughly six months, we were able to accomplish the following:

- Work concurrently on four aspects of developing the prototype. These were its requirements, design and implementation, internal marketing, and management and budget for the project as a whole. Although each of us had different primary responsibilities, we all knew what was going on in the other areas because the conference allowed us to read all the messages being exchanged between everyone. Thus everyone could immediately assess the impacts for their work of what others were doing.
- Work with the customer. We iteratively prototyped the product with its customer and eventual users. The results of prototyping were shared with everyone in the group—not just with those people whose principal responsibility was requirements.
- Work faster. We did not delay communication between us until we had a chance to meet face to face. We communicated continually through the conference.
- Work virtually. We all met only once, after six months, at the demonstration of the finished prototype.
- Work anywhere. The conference was accessible from anywhere on the company's network, so we could continue to take part even when traveling away from our home base. This was particularly important as the project was part-time for most of us.
- Work anytime. We accessed the conference when we had time to spend on the project. We did not have to wade through emails from the other members when we signed onto our computer accounts each day. We could mentally regard the conference as the "project room," which we "entered" when we had time for the project. Again this was important because we were multitasked.
- Work reliably. Every message and piece of information in the conference was stored on the host computer. Nothing got lost. There were no misunderstandings because someone had not received a message.

- Work flat. The project included people at three levels of seniority plus outside contractors. No one paid any attention to these differences. All communication was peer to peer, and decisions were made based on the rightness of the decision, not who made it. The depersonalized, electronic messaging environment has some drawbacks. However, one advantage for technical work is that it's what people have to say, rather than who says it, that becomes important.
- Expand the work. Three months in, we recruited two additional members. We added them to the membership list of the conference. By reading the collected group messages they were immediately able to get up to speed with what was going on.
- Reuse the work. We needed to create an end-of-project document. This was easily assembled by cutting and pasting from what people had written into the conference as they were doing the work.
- Pass the work on. After our prototype demonstration, an engineering group was tasked to continue with a real product. Where was the documentation describing the prototype and the reasons it was like it was? In the conference. We added the key members of the engineering group to the conference and used it to answer their questions over the next couple on months.

The Agile Perspective

What was particularly agile about how we used group conferencing as our core communication process for building the prototype? Of course, we didn't know about agility in 1990, but nonetheless, what we did has in retrospect certain agile elements.

- We shared all information throughout the project group. Being agile means making information available rather than hoarding it. Changing circumstances mean that you never know who is going to need that information, which is why agility requires information to be accessible everywhere. Here it applied to a small group, but the principle is true for whole departments, functions, and enterprises as a whole.
- We worked concurrently on different aspects of the project. The conferencing system held separate threads of messages related to each aspect, but made all these messages available to everyone. Concurrency is a capability required for mastering change.

- We were able to work rapidly, a further capability for mastering change. We avoided delays for meetings and exploited time zone differences. Management worked online continually with us, not needing formal meetings.
- We leveraged resources by including skilled people who would not have been available—due to time pressure—if they had had to travel to project meetings.
- We further leveraged resources by exploiting the knowledge that we had created on the project in preparing our final documentation and in passing the history of the project on to the follow-on engineering group.

What Was Important about Group Conferencing?

We argue that this project represented agile behavior that could not have been possible if we had not used some form of computer networked communication. However, we could always have used email. Why did group conferencing allow us to be more agile than email?

- Email distribution lists would have been clumsier and less easy to use. With a conferencing system, all messages go automatically to every member of the group.
- We might have been more likely not to institute the "all-informed" messaging policy. Senders of messages would have been more likely to think that a certain person didn't really need that message and not send it to them.
- It is very difficult with email to maintain topics or threads of messages related to a subject. Emails related to the same subject are rarely given the same name. To do so requires a discipline that few have. "Reply to" email functions swamp subject lines with a series of "Re:" prefixes.
- Everyone would have been faced with a list of email messages in their communications inbox every morning. We now know that email contributes to a feeling of information overload far more than group conferencing. This is for two reasons. First, each message has to be read and filed or deleted. In a group conferencing system, one selects the messages one wants to read from an index, and one does not have to read all of them. Second, the list of previous messages in a conference topic conveys the context for those messages. Email messages have to be longer to include the context of each message.

- We would have been very unlikely to have preserved one complete record of all the messages that we exchanged for the newly joining members or the follow-on engineering group.

None of these are absolutes. With a great deal of discipline and bother, email could have created the patterns of message distribution and storage that we enjoyed with the group conferencing system. However, we have to say that we severely doubt this. We have never seen people's natural way of using an email system bear much relation, in the important areas of all-inclusiveness, topic indexing, and preservation, to what comes built in with group conferencing.

It is not that email cannot be made to support agile behavior. It is that group conferencing naturally and automatically supports certain aspects of agile communication behavior. Using a group conferencing system makes it more likely that a group will behave in an agile way. To a greater extent than email, group conferencing encourages and supports the following:

- All relevant information accessible throughout a group
- Concurrent working
- Working with large volumes of information rapidly
- Concurrent or later leveraging of the knowledge created by a group

Agile Applications of Group Communication

We have just presented an illustration of group communication underpinning agile behavior. We illustrated this by a case study about developing a prototype information product. There are, however, further ways in which group communication supports agility, referred to at the beginning of this chapter. Here we go into each of these in more detail. In doing so, we build up more evidence of the congruence between group communication and agility.

Enterprise-wide Communication and Knowledge Networking

Project-based applications of group communication are now widespread. We have advanced the case that these are essentially agile. Similar processes can be used to support much larger groups, teams (a subject we address in Chapter 10), whole departments, and even whole enterprises. The principles are much the same. Here are some examples we've seen in a variety of companies.

Note that the following examples illustrate group *communication*, that is, a multiway flow of messages among a group. We are not talking about broadcast publishing of information.

- Product development programs are supported by group conferences. Groups developing a product at different locations coordinate their work and share information in restricted conferences (just a we did in the preceding case). In parallel, open, enterprise-wide conferences allow anyone in the enterprise to contribute ideas, requirements, and competitive analysis. Once the product is developed, open, enterprise-wide group conferences are used to make product technical information available everywhere, to capture and share reviews and customer reactions, as well as maintenance and service tips.

- Key topics in an enterprise's business—marketing, design standards, competitors, customers, opportunities, legislation, projects, and products—are the subject of enterprise-wide group conferences. These perform two important functions. First, they allow information from the outside environment to be captured and disseminated inside. Second, they act as a *knowledge network*. People seeking to answer a question look into the enterprise's directory of group conferences and then go to individual conferences. If the answer isn't there, they post a question. In most cases someone, somewhere in the world, will reply with an answer. Even if an answer isn't forthcoming, browsing a conference identifies people who are working in a relevant area, who can be contacted directly. In this way the enterprise makes its knowledge available to everyone to answer their questions rapidly.

- A new sales team remuneration policy is being developed. A group conference is created in which the vice-president of sales and his staff explain and discuss the detail and implications of the new policy with the sales force. They respond openly to comments and criticisms and take note of consequences and local interpretations. When the policy is implemented, it's on the basis of a thorough testing. Many of the sales force are already aware of what it means for them.

- A senior engineering manager posts his mission, budget, targets, projects, and management structure in a read-only group conference open across his engineering function. He posts his reports to the board the day he makes them. His managers post their reports to him. He and they regularly update this information as situations change simply by pasting new text files into a conference. A parallel conference is open for discussion of what he is saying. It's published policy that no honest comments, however critical, will bring disfavor on the writer.

- Designers and customers (representing eventual users) dialogue in a group conference about the requirements for a new product. The group conference is hosted on an external system to get over both parties' concerns about security. The conference lasts six months, starting with exploration of the concept and purposes of the product and the environment in which it will be used. Its product is a user specification plus elements of the technical specification. The conference archive is used by the engineering group as a reference during product development.

These are enough examples to show how enterprises can use group communication to maintain enterprise-wide (and interenterprise) communication and information. Through these processes, the enterprise makes information available everywhere so that the decisions that they make are not held up by lack of information. The enterprise also uses these methods to capture and recruit the skills and knowledge of all its members and connect with customers. This is agile behavior. We ask you to consider if this could be achieved through email. It is group communication that gives the agile spin.

Group Communication for Entrepreneurship

Enterprise-wide group communication readily creates conditions in which entrepreneurs can thrive. When much of the enterprise's businesses and operations are visible to all employees through internal group conferences, sparks begin to fly. People who would otherwise have a view only of their group or department's work can see what is happening throughout the enterprise. They don't see what is happening through formal internal publications that have been sanitized of any vitality, but through what people are communicating about their work as they do it.

This creates an electronic melting pot. What everyone is doing is visible everywhere. What they are writing about, their business, projects, and customers, is diverse and widespread. This wide-open, living exchange of information about the enterprise is meat and drink to an entrepreneur.

- Thinking of selling in Hungary? Drop a note into a conference run by the Hungarian field office. It'll be faster than a formal manager-to-manager approach. Perhaps someone there can help. Perhaps they'll be enthused enough about your project to spend time offering insight into the Hungarian market for your product. Perhaps, as a result, you can find a niche no one has yet exploited.
- Creating an engineering module? Perhaps there are wider uses for it than anyone thought. Create a conference about it on the "central nervous system." Your module may be the answer to someone's prayers across the globe.
- Have an idea for a new product? Start talking about your idea in a relevant conference. Listen to what people say. Let them help you develop your idea. See who seems really interested. Can they help you with who'd be interested in your proposal? Perhaps they'll want to take part if it gets approved.
- Got a particular expertise that you don't feel is being recognized? Look in the conferences run by other groups who could be interested. Perhaps there's a better market for what you offer.

The network represents a constellation of up-to-the minute opportunities for the entrepreneur. The agile enterprise supports entrepreneurship because it knows that entrepreneurs are the type of people it needs if it is to master change.

Again, we ask if the rich information and communication environment in which an entrepreneur can flourish will come about if people are communicating privately with email rather than publicly with group conferencing.

Group Communication Building Commitment

Here we turn to a very different use of group communication, but also in support of entrepreneurship and thus of leveraging resources. We talked in Part 1 about building commitment to the enterprise and commented that group communication can help to build that commitment. Here we discuss this in more detail.

Experience has shown that being able to communicate across staff levels, functions, and geographies in both formal and informal group conferences can increase the sense of belonging to the enterprise. This happens both at the level of business units and individuals.

Psychologists Lee Sproull and Sara Kiesler, in their 1991 book *Connections,*[1] speak of "subunit drift"—the tendency of business units to lose sight of their membership of the overall enterprise. They make a parallel with the neighborhood. In a neighborhood, interaction based on physical proximity leads people to identify with their neighbors and the neighborhood as a whole. They present evidence that computer-based communication can extend "neighborhood" from the purely physical to the people with whom one is in electronic contact.

One example is an engineering company with offices in Australia and California. The president insisted that all group conference communications about daily events at each site were shared with the other site. The president dismissed claims that what was going on at the other site was irrelevant. He maintained that it was important for each site to be reminded of the existence of the other.

Another example is the Tandem computer company. This company insisted on integrating computer communication networks when it acquired three smaller companies. Not only did this help work information to flow across the now-expanded corporation, but it allowed people everywhere to "meet." The Tandem president wanted people in the newly acquired units to be able to see how long-standing Tandem employees behaved. This was an aid to socialization of the new members, helping them to learn "the Tandem way."

Regarding individuals' commitment to the enterprise, Sproull and Kiesler report a number of research studies.[2]

- In one study, employees of a city government, 90% of whom used email, were surveyed. Individuals' commitment to the employer—willingness to work late hours, their feelings for the employer, and their plans to continue working there—correlated strongly with the amount of email usage. Commitment was not related to the amount they communicated generally (face to face, telephone) nor to grade or seniority. Further studies confirmed that email usage (actually, sending messages rather than receiving them) predicted commitment, and not the other way round.
- In another study, two groups of retirees or near-retirees from a presti-

1. Lee Sproull and Sara Kiesler, *Connections* (Boston: MIT Press, 1991), pp. 150–154.
2. Sproull and Kiesler, Chapter 5.

gious policy research corporation were given the task of developing future retirement policy. One group used email to communicate, the other did not. After six months, the group that used email knew more people, had more interactions, belonged to more subgroups, and felt more involved than their counterparts.

- Another study looked at nonwork-related group conferences within a large corporation. These are "hobby" or "personal interest" conferences unrelated directly to work. Communication analysis of these conferences showed sustained discussion involving people that were remote and unknown (other than through the conference) to each other. Analysis also showed messages related to "groupness." These messages were evidence of participants working at moving from being a set of communicating individuals to being members of a group. Sproull and Kiesler commented, "Membership in any group confers informational and emotional benefits to the member.... These processes are so powerful that people's mental health status is positively related to the number of groups they belong to.... It is plausible, although only a hypothesis at this point, that membership in multiple electronic groups has similar beneficial effects, particularly for people who belong to few face to face groups."

Our experience of enterprise-wide group communication is that there are noticeable and positive effects on commitment to the enterprise. This emerges through an increased sense of community (that is, affiliation with the "group" that is the whole enterprise), belonging, and fellowship. This sense of community does not have to be created through work-related conferences. As Sproull and Kiesler found, the same effects occur in nonwork-related conferences. In the early 1990s, one major technology corporation had over 300 nonwork-related conferences on its internal network. These were permitted because they supported management's aims of creating an inclusive, communicating community of employees.

The agile enterprise seeks to increase the commitment of its people so that their entrepreneurial energies are directed for the benefit of the enterprise. Commitment is also the glue that holds the enterprise together as people work more fluidly in changing roles and tasks, rarely having time to build close face-to-face relationships with or within any single group.

Open Communication

Throughout the examples and descriptions of group communication so far in this chapter, one thing will have become clear: for group communication to successfully support agility, there needs to be open communication within the group, department, or whole enterprise. This is a matter of behavior, not a technical issue.

Not only does open communication underpin the examples of group communication described but it also supports agility. By instituting a policy of open communication, the enterprise demonstrates its trust in its people and asks for commitment as the reciprocal of that trust.

The key elements to create open communication behavior are policy, tools, privacy, culture, practice, and trust, each of which is discussed next.

Policy for Open Communication

A policy to support open communication is that anyone can communicate with anyone else. Such a policy legitimizes that communication can be upward and sideways, across functional boundaries, besides (as it normally is) predominantly downwards, within functional boundaries. Such a policy needs, explicitly or implicitly, to be backed up with a value that no one is criticized or comes into disfavor through honest, polite communication.

Tools for Open Communication

Open communication is aided by the mere fact of group communication. For psychological reasons of anonymity, people experience that the threshold of communicating electronically in a group setting is lower than that of sending an email to an individual or using phone, fax or face-to-face encounters. This means that many people are more likely to communicate using group conferencing than they are using other communication media—including face-to-face.

Privacy Issues

Privacy must be respected. The enterprise needs electronic security to keep private discussions private and internal communications safe from outside eyes. There need to be clear policies about what information can be shared with outsiders.[3] The more secure the internal environment, the more

---

3. In the context of proficiency in partnering, we talked in Chapter 4 about the value to the enterprise of creating a clear and shared view of the value of its knowledge and information and a clear statement of what could and could not be shared with outsiders.

readily information flows within the internal boundary. This is true both of small groups, for whose members knowing with whom information is shared is vitally important, as well as any larger communities.

Cultural Issues

A culture to support open communication, and especially open group, electronically based communication, forms when people find from experience that the following values hold true:

- Information is the enterprise's, and not the personal possession of individuals.
- Valuable information does not have to be exchanged at power lunches—getting it at the right place is the key mandate.
- Information and opinions are never "right" until tested among one's colleagues.
- Knowledge authority, not position authority, is key.
- People take responsibility for what they communicate with others, and it is their responsibility to judge the value of what they receive from others.

Practice of Open Communication

A culture of open communication is, however, the result rather than the cause of people seeing open communication around them. Nothing creates a culture of open communication so much as the practice of open communication. So open communication needs to be kick-started by people in senior positions. Managers who are convinced of the value of open communication have the responsibility to start communicating openly themselves. Here is what a CEO should consider promulgating:

> Here is my email address. If you have something important to say, I want to hear it. You can be sure that I will read every mail that's shorter than one screen. I will not always be able to reply, but will try to. Help me—if you have a question or request, make clear what it is. But don't copy me on mails as a matter of course. If you have something to say, mail it to me directly.

Departmental and group or project managers may publish a similar statement. If they do, they should repay the time investment that people make in writing to them by acknowledging and replying to the majority of messages quickly. Additionally they may want to create group conferences.

If this happens, then their obvious presence in these conferences, as contributors, is important. They also need to refer in their dealing with others to their need to create open communication within their group.

Trust
Trust is the final ingredient needed for open communication. Trust is a major topic in modern business life, and we cannot do it full justice here. However, some things seem clear.

- We note that members of teams, if they are to collaborate, which they must, have to trust each other. When we look at the ingredients for successful teams (as discussed in Chapter 4), we find shared goals important. Extending this to the department or enterprise as a whole, rather than a small number of people in a team, the same is true. Trusting others, especially others who are unknown to you, is helped if you believe them to share your goals.
- Trust is also aided if one's experience is that other people will act in your and the enterprise's best interests with your information, cite the source of valuable information, and, particularly, not use it to harm you.
- Communication builds trust, which also builds communication. Through communicating with people, one calibrates them, obtains a better sense of them, understands what makes them tick. Face-to-face team members have many opportunities to communicate with each other over a long time and thus calibrate each other. At a distance, this calibration needs to happen through electronic communication. But the communication won't happen until trust emerges, and that won't emerge without communication. Hence the best way to start open communication is to start communicating openly, and this needs to be led by senior people.
- Trust is not, however, necessarily the fundamental issue. The fundamental issue is predictability. We usually use the word trust to mean that we believe people act in a predictably good or positive manner. We can just a well believe that people will act in a bad or negative manner. If we believe that correctly, we have learned something important for dealing with them. Trust is only the positive face of predictability: the negative face is just as important. Either way, we build our ability to predict through communication.

Trust pertains not only to open communication within a team, department, or the enterprise as a whole, as we have been discussing it here, but also to knowledge-sharing behavior, which we will discuss in Chapter 9. It is related to empowerment, and to the way people believe that they will be treated as employees. It colors the mutuality of the enterprise and its relationships with its business associates—suppliers, customers, and partners. Open communication both needs trust and helps to create trust, thus contributing to a variety of agile goals. Open communication is thus an underpinning capability of the agile enterprise—one that is difficult and perhaps countercultural to build. Perhaps the softest of the soft things that are so hard to get right. Difficult to justify in business terms. Deeply challenging to many. Probably eroded by rampant "reengineering." But vitally important to the agile enterprise.

Summary

This chapter has been about group communication in the agile enterprise. We have seen that agility is more strongly supported by group communication through technologies such as group conferencing than through one-to-one communication technologies such as email. Group communication builds the conditions for agile work by creating an environment, at any level of the enterprise, in which information and communication flow among people. Group communication also supports entrepreneurship, commitment to the enterprise, and the practice of open, boundaryless, communication that builds trust.

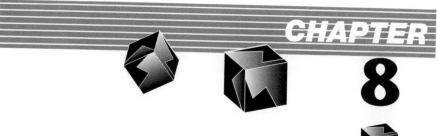

CHAPTER 8

AGILE INTRANET PUBLISHING

In 1995 11% of all large and mid-size companies relied on an intranet. This year, an estimated 70% will.

—BellSouth advertisement, 1997

This chapter is about how the agile enterprise makes information available to all its people through an intranet. Our focus is on broadcasting rich, well-structured, multimedia documents.

We need to distinguish this from the subject of Chapter 7. There the subject was also information being made available across the enterprise. However, in that case, the context was group communication: the exchange of messages between people. This is a very different process and involves different tools and practices to broadcasting information. Although at the end of this chapter we look at the bundling together in intranet systems of publishing and communication functions, the focus for most of this chapter is publishing.

We are talking here also specifically about intranets, that is, about publishing on an internal web. Some of what we have to say is also relevant to Internet publishing, that is, publishing information for public consumption on the external World Wide Web.

Relevance to Agility

In Part 1, when discussing enriching the customer, we said that the agile enterprise needs detailed customer information that must be widely available to its work force.

For mastering change, we said that the agile enterprise requires enterprise-wide information, providing the following:

- The information that reconfigurable individual operations need
- The means to keep everyone informed of the vision, values, mission, and current state of the enterprise

When we discussed leveraging resources, we said that the agile enterprise needs the following:

- To create an enterprise-wide knowledge network
- To keep everyone continually informed

In Chapter 7 we saw how group communication also met these goals. However, group communication is different to publishing information. The difference is that everyone in a group, department, or the whole enterprise can in principle take part in group communication. Rarely, however, does everyone in a group, department, or enterprise publish on an intranet.

Features of Intranets

This is not a book on technology. However, some words on the features of intranets are in order. This is especially necessary as these features are developing rapidly, and we need to make clear what capabilities we are assuming. We are using the word intranet to mean

- internal networks,
- using hypermedia protocols,
- which allow the dissemination of multiply linked documents,
- from anywhere on the network (but typically few sites),
- to anyone whose computer is also on the network and is equipped with the necessary user tools (called a *web browser*),
- where the documents are usually formatted text, images, and graphics, but can also include sound, movies, and animation.

In this context, intranet publishing means the activity of

- creating documents,
- turning them into hypertext mark-up language format,
- linking them with other documents, files, and indexes,
- and making them available to the enterprise on an intranet server.

Intranet user tools (browsers) seem, today, to hold the promise of cross-platform compatibility. That is, users employ more or less the same commands to see documents presented more or less in the same format, regardless of the type of computer or system software that they are using.[1]

Benefits of Intranet Publishing to the Agile Enterprise

Information fuels work in an agile enterprise. The value of this information is not in the *amount* of information available, but in the *relevance, clarity, accessibility,* and *accuracy* of that information. An intranet provides people with just-in-time information: what they need, when they need it, in a flexible format that they can adapt to their specific purposes.

Intranet publishing supports the agile enterprise because it provides answers to information distribution issues. We present the commonest of these next in the Internet style of "frequently asked questions".

How Do We Disseminate Information Rapidly and Keep It up to Date?

Fast-changing, up-to-the-minute information is the lifeblood of the agile enterprise as it senses the accelerating rate of change in its business environment. With intranet publishing, rapidly breaking information can be made available across the enterprise. Updating that information is far quicker than updating paper documents or previous-generation electronic files. And through an intranet publishers know that everyone is seeing the latest generation of that information.

1. We caveat this with the word "today" as competition between vendors may cause some to move their products from such open compatibility to more proprietary standards. If this happens, users with the "wrong" computer or system software will not be able to see the same documents using the same commands as others. Such vendor strategies are, of course, against the customer-enriching principles of agility.

How Do We Get Information from the Outside Inside?

The agile enterprise needs pervasive connections to the environment so that it can sense changes that will affect its business. Intranets allow collections of external links to be created and put in context. Through these links, people inside the enterprise are able to keep themselves up to date on the external environment. Happily, those external information sources are maintained by someone else.

How Do We Know Who Is Going to Need What Information When?

A faster rate of change in the business environment means that you are less likely to know who is going to need what information when. But publishing on an intranet lowers the economic threshold for deciding whether some information is or will be relevant somewhere or sometime. Intranet publishing is showing itself to be a lower-overhead activity than publishing in paper or in traditional electronic formats. Hence a more relaxed attitude can be taken to serving information. The enterprise can afford to maintain more information on its intranet servers than it would otherwise be able to do on paper. Thus it increases the likelihood that someone needing information rapidly will find it.

How Do We Know Where People Need Information?

An agile organization is less likely to know where people are who need specific items of information. This is related to reconfigurability. When operations change their nature, location, and information requirements, it is less likely that the enterprise can predict where any particular item of information is needed. Lack of information resources is avoided by making information more widely accessible on an intranet.

But Won't We Overload People with Too Much Information?

Certainly, information overload is a growing problem. Its solution lies in appreciating the difference between pushing information at people and allowing them to pull it when they need it. Information push happens when people receive letters, memos, faxes, and emails. Information pull happens when people can browse indexes of information sources and select what they want to look at in more detail. Intranet publishing and the underlying hypertext format are the embodiment of information pull. People can progressively access information at greater and greater levels of detail until they find what they want.

Furthermore, through pulling information from intranet pages, users can also select more precise packets of information. The answer that they want may be on one screen. They get to that screen without having to order, or print off, a whole manual, document, or pack.

Do We Give Ourselves a User Training Overhead?

It would be wrong to say that there is no training overhead for using an intranet browser. However, it is small. Many users will have taught themselves how to use these tools through accessing the Internet at work or privately. The tools themselves are (currently) simple and largely standardized across platforms. This allows common training or job aids across the enterprise. Whatever training is required to use an intranet browser is likely to be less than that required to use other information management tools.

How Else Does Intranet Publishing Contribute to Agility?

One of the challenges for the agile organization is to offer products and services that fit niche markets. To do this, it needs to become more market oriented than supply oriented. It also has to act smarter with the information it discovers. Niche markets don't make themselves apparent, at least not to the first entrants.

Acting smarter to discover market niches or products that can satisfy them is related to the way information is handled. It is not only discrete packets of information that are important, but also seeing the patterns and cross references between elements of information. The situation is similar to combining clues in a military intelligence operation. Intranets can help.

1. Intranet pages can collect information that was previously scattered both inside and outside. An inquirer sees a fuller picture in which patterns are more likely to emerge.
2. Browsing a web of hyperlinked documents makes it easier to scan volumes of information than if they were in separate paper or electronic documents.
3. Browsing can be accelerated by using search engines.

These intranet features help people to see a fuller picture not only of information that they knew they wanted, but also of information that they didn't know they wanted. It is more likely that they will *discover* relevant information. Discovering information, while by no means the only thing that an enterprise needs in order to be agile, certainly contributes.

Illustrations of Agile Intranet Publishing

Many examples are available of enterprises publishing information on intranets. Internet and intranet software vendors typically publish customer profiles and case studies of successes with intranets. These are generally available on those vendors' web sites. They show a wide range information published on intranets, such as the following:

- Corporate and departmental white papers
- Document templates
- Policies and procedures
- Standards (policy, quality, technical, personnel)
- Corporate structure and organization chart
- Security information
- Departmental descriptions
- Employee directories
- Health, safety, and environment information
- Library catalogues, with integrated ordering mechanisms
- Product catalogues
- Product user manuals
- Research information shared across R&D groups
- Sales team support information
- Site- and area-specific information
- Travel information

These are valuable uses of intranets—but they are not essentially agile. Were this a book on intranets per se, we would talk more about these uses. However, there are further, more specifically agile uses for intranet publishing. These take advantage of intranet publishing to support agility throughout the enterprise. We identify some agile uses of intranet publishing next.

In the following, we do not say whether the pages should be accessible enterprise wide, department wide, or group or team wide. It may seem natural that some information is less widely accessible than others. The agile preference is that information should be widely rather than narrowly shared. We cannot, however, argue cases in detail in the abstract. But we can advise that the pros and cons of widespread accessibility be carefully weighed from the agile perspective.

Principal Business Customer Information

Being agile means delivering solutions that enrich the customer. When these are business customers, people throughout an agile supplier can better create solutions that fit if they have rich information about the customer at their fingertips. Intranet pages about individual customers can include the following:

- Records of the account responsibilities for that customer
- Details of past business
- Organizational and functional information about the customer
- General intelligence
- Link to or details of the customer's annual report, supplemented with analysis of declared projects and spending patterns
- Analysis of business challenges facing the customer (thus information on how to solve the customer's problems)
- Published articles about or by the customer and about the customer's industry sector in general

The customer may be enlightened enough to recognize that the more the agile supplier knows about its business, the more able it is to provide solutions. In this case more confidential information may be provided openly.

This central collection of customer information is of particular importance when both the agile enterprise and the customer are global. The supplier can delight the customer by being aware of all its worldwide operations. It may spot opportunities that the customer has not seen. If the customer has a similar set of information about the supplier, having a global appreciation of the customer is less a luxury than a necessity.

Competitor Information

Being agile means being ahead of the competition. Intranets allow the agile enterprise to collect and disseminate information from a variety of sources about its principal competitors. This information set may look very much like that prepared for its principal customers, but additionally it can include the following:

- Details of the geography in which the competitor operates
- Formal product competitive analysis
- Ranking of competitors
- Relevant industry news and analysis

Supplier Information

When an agile supplier is part of one's business, it's more than usually important to have a good understanding of that supplier. An agile enterprise can create intranet pages about its principal suppliers. These are likely to cover the types of information described in the preceding two categories.

Reciprocally, the supplier may provide information openly and voluntarily if the relationship is strong. This provides a service to the agile enterprise by allowing its people to select solutions from suppliers with whom it has a relationship. It provides a service to the supplier who gets its capabilities known across the organization.

Partner and Potential Partner Information

We talked in Part 1 about the value to the agile enterprise of drawing up profiles of potential partners. This information can be readily presented on intranet pages, together with details of past and present partnership dealings.

Mass Customer Data

Data collected from surveys and geodemographic analyses of customers at large are often too voluminous to be presented in intranet pages. Furthermore, they are generally stored on specialized data warehouses and accessed through specialist inquiry systems. This makes it unlikely that an intranet can be the front end to mass customer data. This situation may change as data warehousing systems interface with web-based systems. Nonetheless, the agile enterprise can use intranet pages to advise its people of the existence of such data on parallel systems.

Customer Service Information

Agility means providing first-class customer service, either as a product itself or in combination with goods. Many integrated customer service systems exist to support customer-facing staff. They can in principle be based on web technology, but that is not an agility issue. The agility angle is that the information gained from interactions with customers can, through an intranet, be disseminated widely. Consumers of that information will be those responsible for setting strategy, developing product, providing maintenance service, or managing customer accounts.

Market Information

The agile enterprise can assemble on intranet pages both its own market information and links to external sites that complement that internal picture.

Market information will be so various that no particular illustrations here would be meaningful. External sites should be selected to give as wide and multifaceted a picture as possible of the enterprise's markets. Such sites can also include Internet newsgroup discussions.

Legislative Information

Intranet pages can link to external sites providing legislative information to keep the agile enterprise aware of changes in its external business environment. As with all links to external sites, the information on them is maintained by someone else.

Product Information

Information about an enterprise's products is common content for intranet pages. Often, this is the information served publicly on externally facing Internet systems. The agile spin is that this allows people across the enterprise to understand its commercial reason for existence. While not everyone needs an engineer's or salesperson's depth of product knowledge, knowing what and how the enterprise earns its living helps people to identify with what makes it tick. There may also be serendipitous advantages through finding unexpected markets.

Process Information

Information about internal operations and processes is meat and drink to intranet pages. The value to agility of widespread process knowledge is in making it easier to reconfigure operations and processes to meet changes in the business environment.

Project Information

The agile enterprise needs a widespread appreciation of its projects and programs if people are to spot synergies and opportunities for exploiting resources to the full. Intranet publishing provides a way for each project to make itself known across the enterprise.

Confidentiality Rules and Procedures

To protect its own use, the intranet must publish very clear rules governing the confidentiality of the information that it broadcasts. It should also publish confidentiality information more generally. Because all intranet pages are in principle viewable anywhere, they can all be reviewed by people charged with maintaining confidentiality.[2] The stronger the processes that protect the privacy of information within the enterprise's boundary, the more freely information can flow within that boundary.

Organizational Information

To make everyone in the enterprise aware of its culture, status, and opportunities, the agile enterprise publishes a great deal of organizational information for the enlightenment of its staff. This is for two reasons: (1) so that everyone can make decisions in the light of full knowledge of the enterprise's values, mission, strategy, status, and opportunities, and (2) to increase commitment to the enterprise by giving a human face to its people and operations.

Organizational information published for these agile purposes can include the following. Some of this information will be that published publicly on externally facing servers. However, further private information is needed for internal consumption. Additional information will probably be published alongside, for good but not necessarily agile reasons.

---

2. We noted in Chapter 4, in the context of partnership, the value to the enterprise of creating a clear view of what of its information could be shared with whom and under what conditions.

Corporate level

- Annual report
- Daily and historical stock prices
- Mission value and goal statements
- Company history and important milestones
- Summary organization and function chart, linking to departmental pages, including pictures and profiles of senior corporate managers
- Key strategies (including agility)
- Press releases (on the day of release, please)
- Public statements made by senior managers
- Remuneration policies and procedures and example of calculation (when these reflect value added to the enterprise)[3]
- Internal job opportunities and calls for staff to join temporary teams

Departmental Level

- Departmental and functional descriptions, including pictures, profiles and messages from senior departmental managers
- Departmental missions, opportunities and strategies
- Departmental projects and programs
- Detail of remuneration policies per department
- Other departmental versions of corporate material

Employee Information

It is a matter of policy whether the enterprise wishes to give every employee the opportunity to create his or her own personal intranet page. There are four potential benefits.

1. There is psychological evidence that being able to communicate with others builds commitment to groups.[4] Similar display of self on an intranet may have the same effect.

2. Purely practically, employee contact details are readily found.

3. Employees can present profiles of their skills and career development

---

3. Visible remuneration policies, based on value-added performance, are part of creating an entrepreneurial environment.

4. Joseph E. McGrath, *Groups: Interaction and Performance* (Englewood Cliffs, NJ: Prentice Hall, 1984).

aspirations. This helps the right people to be selected for full-time job moves or part-time membership on temporary groups and teams.

4. Such pages can hold pictures of the individuals. This is beneficial: it gives a face and context to people with whom others may interact remotely without having met.

The downside is the space taken up on corporate information servers, potentially uneven treatment of modest individuals, and offensiveness to people from cultures that do not approve of individual display.

Training and Development Information

The agile enterprise's work force needs training and development to acquire the new skills necessary to adapt to changing task requirements. Intranet pages of training and development courses and opportunities will contribute to this goal, bringing a wide range of materials to individuals' attention. The more agile solution, however, is for training and development materials to be deliverable through the intranet itself, for example, downloadable courseware, self-assessment tests, and job and performance aids. Other forms of interactive distance learning available through an intranet are the subject of Chapter 11.

Responsible Agile Publishing

One danger of intranet publishing is that authors or publishers can take their view about what is appropriate content or presentation style from the World Wide Web. With no adjudication of content and a wide range of people publishing on the web, material found there is very diverse. Just because something is on the web does not mean that its style is appropriate for an internal site. People reading material on an intranet are being paid by the enterprise. Their time is valuable, and intranet publishers must do all they can to allow readers to find valuable content with minimum effort.

This consideration has to balance what we have been saying above about the range of information that can, from an agile perspective, be valuably published. We are not calling for a free-for-all publishing explosion. Certainly, agility calls for more rather than less information to be published. However, each page has to be published in a disciplined and responsible manner. This discipline has to be exercised by individual publishers across the enterprise.

This is consistent with agile management style. People are given more information with which to do their jobs and make decisions, and the enterprise manages in a hands-off manner. In turn, people in whom trust has been demonstrated act in a responsible manner.

Considerations of Responsibility for Intranet Publishers

Responsible publishing means that individuals, groups, and departments take the following view:

- We owe it to ourselves and our enterprise to publish professionally.
- We owe it to our readers that the information that we publish be accurate, not misleading, not exaggerated, and constantly maintained.
- We owe it to the enterprise to reinforce readers' expectations that everything found on an internal source is accurate and current.

It's not difficult to imagine the loss of confidence that can occur if readers learn that intranet information should always be treated with suspicion. This may be a legitimate view of the Internet. However, an intranet's readers are co-workers, and the intranet has cost time and money to establish.

Responsible publishers need to ask themselves the following questions:

- What is our purpose in publishing? (Answers to this come from considering the illustrations of agile intranet publishing, given previously.) Do we have anything to say that is unique? Do we have the time and resources to say it well?
- Do we commit to maintain the material (content, dates, links, and addresses) in these pages so that it is always current and accurate?
- Can we create (or distill) information-intensive content that meets the time constraints of our readers? Is our material consistent with an "attention economy"? Or are we simply uploading publicity puffs and sales brochures?
- Is the content ours to publish and are we the authoritative source of this information? Should we publish this or should someone else?

Can and should we take responsibility for providing the enterprise as a whole with the definitive content about a particular topic?

- Have we surveyed the Internet to provide links to external information that complements the internal picture that we are presenting?
- What is the value to our readers of this material? What might our readers do as a result of having access to the material? What opportunities for exchange of information or collaboration are we offering them?
- Do we know what viewing tools (browsers) we can assume that everyone has access to and can use readily?
- Do we understand the corporate security rules for publishing and does the intended material comply? Do we understand the corporate style and how this will apply to our material?
- Do we understand from where these pages will be linked in the corporate intranet?
- Do we have a plan to test the material with a representative audience before publication?
- Have we got the right people on our team (content providers, web stylists and editors, web technology advisers)?
- Have we taken and followed up on advice offered from specialist resources?

Role of Intranet Advisory Function

It is typical for intranet publishing to fall under the aegis of an existing corporate publications function. Such a function has usually overseen the publication of internal (and often external) publications for decades. We can presume that within a corporate publications function something we can call an *intranet advisory function* will be formed.

The role of this function is not and cannot be to publish all the information on the corporate intranet. Rather, the role is to set in place the systems whereby departments, projects, and groups can publish their own information. This means moving from a doing function to a management or leadership function. This is consistent with an agile management style in which people are given responsibility, but also information in order to act responsibly.

In this light, the key roles of an intranet advisory function are as follows:

- Being a center of expertise for web publishing, including providing training both face to face and via the intranet. Creation of exemplar sites. Creation of organizational style guides, templates, and approved corporate logos and graphics.
- Establishing the approved list or total portfolio of viewers and tools in use across the enterprise; definition of a lowest common denominator suite.
- Maintaining of links to external web resources: style guides, software, innovations.
- Establishing, promulgating, and supervising intranet security policies and procedures.
- Maintaining the enterprise-wide web linking structure and creating meaningful indexes and contents lists of pages published enterprise wide; selecting and maintaining search engines.
- Maintaining archives of current and past intranet sites.
- Liaison with corporate officers regarding the value of the intranet; collecting value examples from across the organization.

Intranets and Collaboration

So far we have been talking about intranets in their role as a channel for publishing rich, well-structured information. This is the role that intranets have inherited from the World Wide Web. However, there is a new and emerging role for intranets, which has to do with supporting communication.

We talked about group communication in Chapter 7. We noted that the traditional group communication technologies, principally group conferencing, are now being bundled with intranet systems. The implication is that alongside publishing (broadcasting) prepared information, intranets now support communication—exchange of messages between individuals or within groups. Group and person-to-person communications are now becoming tightly integrated with intranets' publishing function. On an intranet web page, a selectable link can present the reader wither either a blank email form or entry to an internal group conference.

There are some powerful implications of the coming together of publishing and communication within intranet systems. These greatly increase the potential for collaboration within the enterprise. We give some examples next of using the collaborative power of the intranet, as well as its publishing power, to your benefit.

- Whatever you're publishing, use an embedded email address to ask for comments and questions. If patterns emerge in the questions, then publish a list of "Frequently Asked Questions" (FAQs) about the material.
- If you're publishing research information or pages about a newly breaking topic, consider creating a group conference about the topic and putting a link to that conference within the page. Then people have something to say about your topic can engage in discussion with you and other similarly interested people.
- If you're publishing material for motivational reasons, to let people across the organization know of positive events or programs, then create internal conferences alongside the published pages. In these, people can discuss their reaction to the material, inquire about what is happening in their geography, and give you feedback on the effects it is having.
- Similarly, if you're publishing resources, such as tools, standards, or templates, use associated conferences for discussion of these, to generate lists of FAQs and to let peers help each other to learn how to use them.
- As a manager of a distributed, multilocation team, use intranet publishing to inform your team of mission, goals, status, events, composition, administration, deadlines, and milestones. Use associated group conferences as your electronic workplace, available around the world and across every time zone.

Summary

Intranets are a valuable technology for the agile enterprise. Through intranet publishing, the agile enterprise can handle the greater amount of information that it needs to disseminate with less overhead and less danger of information overload. There are a number of specific examples of agile intranet publishing, where the material published supports agile principles and strategies. The greater amount of information that the agile enterprise publishes means, however, more discipline and responsibility from individual publishers.

Future developments of intranet technology will see an increasingly close link between its publishing function and the support of communication. This creates exciting new collaborative potential within the agile enterprise.

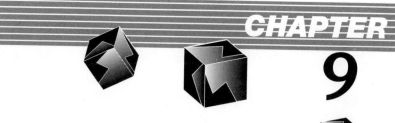

AGILE KNOWLEDGE
MANAGEMENT

Knowledge is of two kinds. We know a subject ourselves, or we know where we can find information about it.

—Samuel Johnson, 1709–1784

In this chapter we describe how the agile enterprise manages its knowledge. As we write, knowledge management is one of the hottest topics in corporate strategy. Conferences and articles proliferate. Prestigious companies announce major investments. Technology vendors calculate impressive returns on investment. At the same time, much rebadging has been going on. Approaches once called reengineering, networking, document management or groupware are now called knowledge management.

Besides the current excitement, however, the widespread interest in knowledge management is important to agility. Knowledge management, independently of but in parallel with agility, has created a focus on leveraging the enterprise's knowledge for competitive advantage. Knowledge management systems may reasonably be regarded as "knowledge multipliers"[1]—particularly important to agile enterprises. However, agility has certain rather special requirements for knowledge management. These requirements are not necessarily comfortable for people who believe that knowledge management is about distributing information.

Relevance to Agility

The agile principle of leveraging resources, described in Part 1, demands a strategy of exploiting skill and knowledge assets in the enterprise. This strategy requires that skill and knowledge assets be

- identified and valued,
- made accessible everywhere,
- capable of being captured,
- capable of being developed.

We showed in Chapter 7 how people's skill is mobilized through group communication networks. People with valuable skills can exhibit themselves to others and communicate with others across the enterprise. The remaining knowledge aspects, however, are similar to many strategies calling themselves knowledge management.

The agile enterprise also manages knowledge explicitly because its products incorporate more knowledge than standardized, commodity, mass-produced products. We saw in Part 1 that, in enriching the customer, the agile enterprise creates customized solutions. The difference between these customized solutions and commodity products is the amount of knowledge that they embody. They must embody more knowledge about the customer and the customer's business if they are to be solutions. They must entail more knowledge about the marketplace if they are to be niche products. Moreover, an agile enterprise produces more solutions per year than a nonagile enterprise. So not only is the amount of knowledge needed to create each solution greater, but also there are more solutions to be created.

---

1. Military command and control systems are developed on the premise that they are a "force multiplier," that through their coordination function they amplify the effectiveness of individual units and equipments. Similarly, knowledge management systems can be seen as "knowledge multipliers." That is, they make the enterprise's knowledge more effective by getting it to the right place at the right time.

Agility is firmly aligned with ideas of the knowledge-based, postindustrial economy. As we said in Part 1, agility particularly recognizes that a knowledge-based economy is increasingly important to developed countries. This is because the know-how to produce standardized commodity products has been successfully exported to low-wage economies.

Agility also speaks practical sense to the businessperson. The following quote from The Agility Forum's "Agile People Development Group Newsletter" speaks volumes:

> CEOs, when asked how much of the knowledge which is available to the company is actually used, responded "only about 20%" (Gottlieb Duttweiler Foundation). Yet if this figure represented average utilization of production capacity, it would only be acceptable to the most foolhardy CEOs.[2]

What will concern us particularly here is the special requirement that agility has of knowledge management. What was valuable knowledge one year may not be valuable the next year. The half-life of valuable knowledge in the agile enterprise is shorter than that in the nonagile enterprise. For this reason, the focus for agile knowledge management (and thus of this chapter) is not so much on what you do with knowledge once you have it, but rather on the processes that *create* knowledge and how it is *valued*.

Common Views of Knowledge Management

The core issue of knowledge management is to place knowledge under management remit to get value from it—to realize intellectual capital. This intellectual capital can be regarded as a major determiner of the difference between a company's book price and the total value of its stock. For a successful company, this difference can be considerable, representing the difference between the way the company is seen by accountants and by the market. It has long been possible to measure the financial value of the enterprise's physical assets. Today, specialists are offering ways to measure the financial value of its knowledge assets. When there is consensus on how to put knowledge on the balance sheet, we can expect far more precise management methods than exist currently.

2. *Agility Forum Agile People Development Group Newsletter* (Bethlehem PA: Iacocca Institute) February, 1996.

Nonetheless, process frameworks are now emerging for knowledge management. Typically, they take the form of the following steps.

1. Capture knowledge
2. Organize and store knowledge
3. Disseminate or distribute knowledge
4. Utilize or apply knowledge

Technologies are readily recruited. In the same period that knowledge management has become fashionable, so has intranet publishing. This has resulted in much crosstalk between the two. Much of what we talked about in Chapter 8 about intranet publishing is called knowledge management. The argument is that if corporate publications, sales packs, customer information, product information, organizational information, and so on, represent knowledge, then capturing, organizing and storing, and disseminating that knowledge throughout the enterprise on intranet web pages is knowledge management.

This relatively simple view of knowledge management is not, however, enough for the agile enterprise, for two principal reasons:

1. There is insufficient emphasis on the processes that create knowledge.
2. Knowledge is devalued by strategies that confuse it with information. While the agile enterprise certainly requires processes that disseminate information, it particularly needs processes to manage what we can call real knowledge. It needs these because much more of its business is based on real knowledge.

To deal with these objections to how knowledge management is commonly regarded, we need to explain some characteristics of real knowledge.

Characteristics of Real Knowledge

There is no easy way to define knowledge. One-liners remain feebly abstract ("Knowledge is usable information"). Encyclopedic treatises dismay the reader with detail. Here we will pragmatically describe knowledge by those operational characteristics that we must appreciate if we are to capture, store, and utilize knowledge for agility.

- *Knowledge is a human capability.* Knowledge is a human capability rather than the property of an inanimate object such as a book or computer record. It is a personal capability like a skill, experience, or intelligence: a capability to do or to judge something, now or in the future. This capability can be acquired by someone as a result of reading, seeing, or listening to something. What is read, seen, or heard is not the knowledge; rather, it is the material through which knowledge may be transferred.[3] This means that knowledge management tools don't manage knowledge, but capture, organize, store, and transmit source material from which someone may acquire knowledge.
- *Knowledge is the result of a personal transform.* Whether someone does acquire knowledge depends on an interaction between that person and the source material. Material, for example a treatise on bird migration patterns, that transfers knowledge to some people, for example ornithologists, fails to transfer it to other people, for example your authors. The transform depends on relevance, context, and how the material is structured. Note that we say "Here's the information you wanted about...." but not "Here's the knowledge about...." In our language we recognize that knowledge is the result of a personal transform.
- *Knowledge is generative.* Having knowledge means having an appreciation at the level of a map or a web, rather than a nondimensional data point or a one-dimensional fact. It means that one can explain, explore, and apply interpolations and abstractions. Most importantly, having knowledge means that one can generate new appropriate statements about a subject, not just reproduce the statements that were received.[4]

---

3. Even though we make this theoretical distinction between knowledge and potentially knowledge-bearing materials, we shall now revert to the more usual use of the term and regard the materials as synonymous with the knowledge that they may contain.

4. To be a licensed London black cab driver, candidates have to pass an examination that takes two to three years' preparation. This tests their ability to describe the location of every street and major building in Greater London and to construct the best route from any place to any other place under different traffic conditions. London cabbies call this qualification "The Knowledge."

We illustrate the differences between data, information, and knowledge in Figure 9–1.

- *Knowledge is elaborate.* While one talks of "a piece of information," one refers to "a body of knowledge." This body is an extensive, organized set of information. It comes in large packets—not in sound bites. People acquire knowledge (learn) over weeks and months rather than minutes and hours. It devalues knowledge to confuse it with less elaborate information.
- *Knowledge about work is best acquired through work.* Knowledge acquired in and through working has not been abstracted and

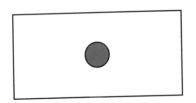

Data

0 - dimensional
A fact
Reproducible

GREAT WESTERN RAIL SERVICE
DEP. PADDINGTON 4.54 ARR. SWINDON 5.45

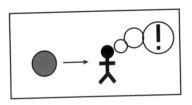

Information

1 - dimensional
A difference that make a difference
A relevant item of data
Reproducible

"The train I want leaves at 4:54."

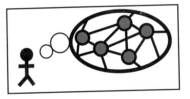

Knowledge

2 - dimensional
A human capability to act or decide
A web or map or body of information
Generative

"Trains are machines that travel on rails.
Trains run to a schedule.
If I miss the 4:54 I will have to take a later train.
Because trains only stop at stations,
I will have to drive home from the station.
I need £1 for the car park.
I will be home about 6:30 if I can catch the 4:54."

Figure 9–1 Illustrating Data, Information, and Knowledge.

reshaped as it is when presented in a book, manual, or course. One less translation means one less layer to deconstruct to map the knowledge to one's own perspective.[5]

- *Knowledge is both explicit and tacit.* Explicit knowledge is what can be put into manuals and methodologies. It can be easily articulated and thus captured, stored, and disseminated. Additionally, however, there is tacit knowledge. Tacit knowledge is personal knowledge held in people's heads. It is about beliefs, assumptions, opinions, perspectives, and values. By definition, it is unformalized and unarticulated. We would likely say that it's what people really know. Because it is in people's heads, it is difficult to put it into manuals and methodologies.

  Since the late 1980s, Ikujiro Nonaka of Tokyo University has argued, influentially, that knowledge is created through the interaction of tacit and explicit knowledge.[6] He comments that the capability to recognize and deal with tacit knowledge is a Japanese strength underlying their economic performance.

  The difference between explicit and tacit knowledge is illustrated in the common case when enterprises set out to capture work processes in documented methodologies. These aim to get the knowledge from "people who have done it" documented and available across the enterprise. The problem is that these methodologies typically only document the explicit or formal task elements. Rarely do they document the tacit or informal knowledge reflecting the thinking that actually took place. Hence they do not capture the dynamics, uncertainties, insights, interactions, and deliberations of the original work process. While they may set down the what, they usually fail to set down the why. Thus they fail to capture the reality of how. Documented methodologies, then, usually represent *know-what* rather than *know-how*.

Our discussion shows that it is dangerous to confuse real knowledge with information and to believe that by disseminating formalized, explicit knowledge one is engaged in real knowledge management. What is now emerging, however, is a more human-centered view of knowledge management, which is better aligned with agility and with the characteristics of real knowledge. We describe this next.

5. London cabbies learn "The Knowledge" by driving the streets of London on motorbikes.
6. Ikujiro Nonaka and Hirotaka Takeuchi, *The Knowledge-creating Company: How Japanese Companies Create the Dynamics of Innovation* (Oxford: Oxford University Press, 1995).

Five Operating Principles

Brook Manville and Nathaniel Foote of the McKinsey & Co. consulting firm offer valuable and concise advice in the form of five operating principles for knowledge management. These operating principles are about real knowledge and, although not written in the context of agility, are keys for agile knowledge management.[7]

1. Knowledge-based strategies have to start with providing value to the customer.
2. Knowledge-based strategies must link to performance measures: they need to show explicit value, rather than being generally "good for the company."
3. A knowledge-based strategy is not about managing knowledge; it is about nurturing people with knowledge.
4. Organizations leverage knowledge through networks of people who collaborate—not networks of technology that interconnect.
5. People networks use knowledge through pulling it when they need it, not by having it pushed at them.

We take these principles as a guiding framework for outlining an agile approach to knowledge management.

Validated on the Basis of Customer Value

Agility is rooted in providing value to the customer; hence an agility perspective strongly endorses Manville and Foote's first principle. Agile knowledge management begins with identifying the knowledge in the enterprise that adds value to the customer. Because this is so important, we talk about an agile approach to valuing knowledge separately in the next section.

Validated through Performance Measures

The second of Manville and Foote's principles refers to tracking the value of knowledge management and describing its impact on traditional performance measures. The value of explicitly managing (capturing, storing, and

7. Brook Manville and Nathaniel Foote, "Strategy As If Knowledge Mattered," *Fast Company*, April/May 1996.

disseminating) the valued knowledge needs to be demonstrated. Is the knowledge management exercise paying its way, or would things just as well have been left as they were?

Nurturing People with Knowledge

This principle refers to the issue of tacit and explicit knowledge already described. Explicit knowledge (as with a documented methodology) is easy to extract and manage. Tacit knowledge is much more difficult to extract and to manage. Unfortunately, tacit knowledge is not only a key part of knowledge creation; it is more valuable in itself than explicit knowledge. People will continue to be the source of tacit knowledge and thus people will be pivotal in the creation of valuable knowledge. From the agility perspective, we now see further reason to value the people in the enterprise and their skills.

Knowledge Is Leveraged through Networks of People Who Collaborate

People collaborating create and use knowledge. All technology can do is to provide them with the means to collaborate at a distance or to access knowledge materials. In a second article on knowledge management,[8] Manville and Foote talk about communities of practice—informal networks of people who do the same or similar kinds of work. They point out that the human or collaborative ties within these communities are part of knowledge management. These ties create the collaborative environment in which knowledge is shared without concern for loss and used without worrying about "not invented here."[9] These communities of practice, in that they openly share and collaborate, have much in common with real teams, as discussed in Chapter 4.

People Networks Utilize Knowledge by Pulling What They Need

Communities of practice represent the demand for knowledge—utilizing it to accomplish their task. As Manville and Foote point out, successful knowledge management strategies are demand led rather than supply led.

---

8. Brook Manville and Nathaniel Foote, "Harvest Your Workers' Knowledge," *Datamation*, July 1996.

9. Manville and Foote comment that downsizing very effectively extinguishes knowledge sharing.

The value of knowledge is released only when it is put to use, not while it is sitting in a repository. Thus demand and utilization, rather than supply and storage, determine value. Similarly, a demand philosophy is important in disseminating materials. They need to be made accessible to people, not distributed at them. Manville and Foote comment, as we did in Chapter 7, that pushing information at people is a cause of information overload.

Valuing Knowledge for Agility

Because knowing the value of what you know or need to know is so important for agility, we outline here an approach to valuing knowledge specifically designed for the agile enterprise.

Broad Categories of Knowledge for the Agile Enterprise

The agile enterprise should assess the knowledge it possesses under the following categories:

- Knowledge required to produce goods and services that customers value, including core competencies
- Knowledge about customers, customer relationships, the marketplace, and the wider business environment
- Knowledge about critical internal processes, including how to be agile
- Other knowledge

Questions That Reveal Value

Valuing this knowledge can proceed from the following simple questions:

- What would the impact be on your customers if you did not have this knowledge?
- What would the impact be on you if this knowledge were in a competitor's enterprise and not in yours?
- If you did not have this knowledge, would customers switch to your competitors who did? If not, what additional knowledge do you have that keeps them?
- Is this knowledge already in the competitor's enterprise as well as in yours? If it is, what additional knowledge lets you retain customers?

- How much would you charge to sell this knowledge to a competitor?
- How much would you be willing to pay for this knowledge if you did not have it?

What's the Time Horizon?

Using the outlined approach, a ranked inventory of the valued knowledge in the enterprise can be created. However, this is a static inventory. The agile enterprise needs to think about how the value of this knowledge may change by asking the following questions:

- What now looks like enduring knowledge?
- What now looks like knowledge past its use-by date?
- What now looks like breaking knowledge that will be increasingly valuable?

And other questions to ask:

- What have we now learned about knowledge that we don't possess but can predict that we will need if we are to deliver value to our customers in a turbulent business environment?
- When we have valuable knowledge, how are we going to get it known across the enterprise? (We talk about knowledge acquisition in Chapter 11.)

Arising Actions

Following the preceding simple steps provides insight into the knowledge resources of the enterprise and leads to identifying the most valued knowledge. There are then three arising actions.

1. Manage the most valuable knowledge—capture, store, and disseminate it to people who can reuse it. We don't say much about this here, since many sources offer advice on capturing, storing, and disseminating knowledge. However, at the end of this chapter we show how intranets can underpin knowledge webs. Nonetheless, in managing this knowledge it is important not to confuse it with information. Is the knowledge elaborate and based on work, rather than an abstraction from work? Is it only explicit (know-what) or both explicit and tacit (know-how)?

2. Protect that knowledge. We have seen twice already in this book the importance of protecting intellectual property, first in the context of being prepared for partnering, and second in the context of internal publishing in intranets. Now we see that valuing knowledge, as described here, provides the basis for deciding its confidentiality. Hence a product of agile knowledge management is not just a view of the knowledge that must be captured and mobilized. Another key output is the *Intellectual Property Asset Inventory,* which ascribes a level of confidentiality to each item of valued knowledge.

3. Analyze the most valued knowledge to learn how to create new knowledge in future. We emphasize again that the agile enterprise needs to understand the processes that create its knowledge, because the half-life of agile knowledge is short. Studying how most valued knowledge was created in the past will be highly instructive.

- How did these most valued knowledge items come about: invention, insight, serendipity, strategic initiative, from buying the knowledge owners, from studying a competitor, from interaction with customers, from partners?

- In what functions was it created: research, engineering, marketing, the sales force, management, product development, service—or a combination of these?

- Through what processes was it created: individuals' work, functional teamwork, cross-functional teamwork?

Answering these questions may lead to surprises. It's very possible that valued knowledge will be found to have been created in multidisciplinary teamwork on customer problems over a long period, rather than in a research lab. Whatever the answer, however, knowing how valued knowledge was created leads to greater understanding of how, in the enterprise's own context, valued knowledge can be created in the future.

Agile Knowledge Management Based on Group Conferencing

In the following paragraphs, we outline an approach to knowledge management based on group conferencing technology by means of a case study. We present this because it is a good example of knowledge being created, captured, and reused. In this case, knowledge was managed in a group conferencing environment.[10] Group conferencing has particular benefits for knowledge management.

- A group of people communicating is the ideal seed bed for knowledge creation. In group communication (the process that group conferencing supports), we see the interaction of tacit and explicit knowledge that Nonaka identifies as leading to knowledge creation. When people are working with one another to solve a problem, each must make his or her beliefs and assumptions (tacit knowledge) explicit for these to be available to others. Thus tacit knowledge is surfaced and made explicit through group dialogue. The Lotus Institute, part of the Lotus groupware company, explains that tacit knowledge is usually shared through conversation and shared experience, in situations where people are part of a community sharing a common context. They explain that, when knowledge is explicit, collaboration technologies like group conferencing support capture, organization, and dissemination. When knowledge is tacit, these technologies support the personal interaction required for it to be created, made explicit, and shared.[11]
- More usually that not, group communication takes place within a culture of collaboration and sharing and a shared context. This is the culture required if people are to share knowledge with their colleagues. It is most likely to be found within a team. Thus we point to teams as prime knowledge-creating units. It may also, however, be found within a community of practice of any size.
- People communicate in groups all the time without using a group conferencing system. Why do we point to group conferencing particularly? There are two reasons.

  1. Group conferencing automatically creates a record of the messages that people exchange with each other. Nothing is lost. Face-to-face interactions, unless extensively minuted, rarely capture the whole dialogue and thus expressions of tacit knowledge. Other communi-

10. For what we mean by group conferencing, see Chapter 7.

11. Michael H. Zack and Michael Serino, *Knowledge Management and Collaboration Technologies* (Cambridge, MA: Lotus Development Corporation, 1996).

cation technologies are either one to one (phone, email) or do not create a record of the exchanges. As was pointed out to us about audio and video conferencing, "these tools leave no footprint."

2. Group conferencing allows people to communicate at a distance. This makes it a good fit for multidisciplinary work situations, where people of different skills and knowledge interact. The interaction between different disciplines is important. It makes people explain ideas that are common in their discipline but not in others'. Thus they articulate assumptions and beliefs: tacit knowledge.

- Group conferencing is a pull, not push, technology. Its use, rather than email, minimizes information overload.

To summarize, from what we know about tacit and explicit knowledge, we can say that knowledge is most readily created in group communication. For the knowledge created to be preserved for reuse, it needs to be recorded, and group conferencing automatically records group dialogue. Hence agile knowledge management strategies, which must be concerned foremost with the processes that create knowledge, need to be based in group conferencing.

Example of Group Conferencing in Knowledge Management

In 1991 two of us took part in a major proposal made by an international information and communications systems company to a U.S. aerospace manufacturer. The proposal was to provide systems and services for the development of a new commercial aircraft. New integrated, concurrent development techniques were to be applied.

We took on the role of creating process for the concurrent working of the proposal team itself, which eventually numbered 140 people across eleven U.S. states and six countries. We chose group conferencing as the process to integrate the proposal activities. We designed the conferencing and collaboration environment to achieve the following:

- Enable cross-functional collaboration among the 10 specialist skill groups in the proposal team, allied account teams, and (our) partner companies.
- Demonstrate to the customer that conferencing would support concurrent development.

- Coordinate a team activity that was geographically distributed and reduce the cost and inconvenience of contributors' travel.

If you had looked at the electronic workspace at the height of the proposal development, you would have seen the following:

- Over 90% of the team's communication was taking place within group conferences or copied into the conferences. Person-to-person email was the exception.
- Each of the 10 skill groups was working within its own conference but browsing other groups' conferences.
- Members of each skill group were cross-posting notes that they felt were important to other groups' conferences.
- Material from all conferences was being used to create the emerging proposal document.

Concurrent Knowledge Management

What we helped to create for this proposal was a system for *concurrent knowledge management.*[12] The team generating the knowledge was the team that used the knowledge in their work, managing it as they went. The knowledge was captured as it was created using the same tools as were used in the work. Knowledge about the work was used as soon as it was shared in the work.

Archival Knowledge Management

What happened after the proposal was submitted is a telling story about *archival knowledge management.* Senior management created a separate task force to genericize the final proposal document into a proposal template for aerospace bids, similar to the process of documenting methodol-

12. Knowledge management strategies commonly take the view that knowledge management is something that happens once a piece of work has been finished and before the next piece of work has started. Knowledge captured at time A is organized and stored in some archive or repository and made available to another group of people at a later time B. This is the form of knowledge management employed by enterprises that transfer process into documented methodologies. In contrast to this *archival* view of knowledge management, we believe it is also important to focus on *concurrent* knowledge management. This takes place when knowledge is captured, organized, disseminated, and utilized by the same people in a continuous, seamless, concurrent process. The community that generates the knowledge is the community that applies the knowledge, creating immediate value for the enterprise.

ogy discussed earlier. This was not a success. The result of the proposal work was still there, but it was not on its own accessible. Particularly, nothing in it gave any clue to why the team had chosen any of the solutions that they proposed.

Soon after, however, we became involved with another aerospace customer, this time in Europe. Again, we were part of a team bidding to support a concurrent development strategy. One of the first things we did was to open the group conferencing archive created by the earlier proposal team. The new team read the conferences. They understood not only the details of the proposal that the original team had created, but why they had done it and what went on while they were doing it. From the captured dialogue they could identify with the decisions, disagreements, discussions, and even the emotions that were flowing at critical points. They were able to abstract key points from the captured dialogue of the earlier proposal. These were both points that they already knew that they needed answers to and points that they didn't know that they needed answers to.

Reusing Knowledge from Group Conferences

The second, later team was able to reuse knowledge that the earlier team had created because their task was much the same as the original team's. In Manville and Foote's words, they were a similar community of practice. Because they had much the same perspective, they found a familiar structure. However, the knowledge in that archive might not have been accessible to someone looking at it from a different perspective.

For example, the original team had proposed that the client use the computer company's established phase review process. The way in which it would be applied was discussed in a number of conferences, as it was applicable to a number of different aspects of the proposal. There was no one conference called "phase review process." Hence someone interested in learning how the phase review process was presented in this proposal would not have found that laid out in one conference and would have had to browse all the conferences to find mention of it.

The answer to making conference archives reusable by people with a different perspective is found in today's HTML-based int*net[13] authoring tools. Their essential characteristic is to allow documents to be hyper-

---

13. We're using the construction "int*net" in this book to refer generically to both the Internet and intranet. When we mean either of these specifically, we say so.

linked. The World Wide Web hyperlinks documents across the Internet. An intranet hyperlinks documents across an internal network. The same technology can be used to hyperlink messages within group conference archives. This turns the content of the group conference into a web of knowledge. This web of knowledge allows a number of different views to be taken of it. It does not only support the creators' views, but it allows someone with a different perspective to find what they need.

For example, someone looking at a hyperlinked archive from the perspective of "phase review process" would find those words highlighted as a link in a conference message. Then they could follow links from that mention to all other mentions and links to related subjects. At each link, they would be able to read what people were saying to each other about the phase review process. They could follow these threads of discussion, building up an extensive and elaborate picture of how the phase review process had been discussed and presented.

The HTML-based tools that allow this relinking are, of course, the same tools that are used to author int*net documents. Indeed, the original group conferences may have been run on an intranet web conferencing system. Thus intranets emerge as important technologies for knowledge management, as described next.

Importance of Intranets for Agile Knowledge Management

We said earlier that a spatial analogy of knowledge is a web: a set of connections between items of information that form an organized body. Within this body of knowledge, it is connections as much as items of information that represent knowledge and allow people holding that knowledge to make generative statements.

Thanks to intranets, this spatial analogy can be represented in the organization of documents and files comprising knowledge material. Intranet authoring tools allow multiple items to be linked together in a knowledge web, not only the archive of one group conference, but linked content from one archive to another. And such webs can hold items of information, linked and organized in the context of the tacit-rich knowledge created in dialogue.

Thus an intranet is a key tool for an enterprise's knowledge management strategy.

- Intranets may be the host technology for group conferences, in which real knowledge is created and captured and used concurrently by the people creating the knowledge.
- Intranets allow real knowledge, captured in group conferencing archives, to be relinked and made accessible for later reuse by people with multiple perspectives.
- Intranets allow multiple conference archives and other items of information to be linked together in an enterprise-wide knowledge web.
- This knowledge web is readily extensible because intranets make it easy to link in new items.
- The intranet readily supports contents listing and indexing that allows the knowledge web to be presented to users.
- The intranet then makes each item in the knowledge web accessible across the organization, letting users, teams, or communities of practice pull that knowledge when they need it.

Summary

The agile enterprise needs to manage real knowledge because much of its business is knowledge based. Real knowledge is different from information. It also includes tacit knowledge as well as the explicit knowledge that most knowledge management strategies concentrate on. The agile enterprise particularly needs to create knowledge, because in a changing business environment the half-life of valuable knowledge is short. It must also value the knowledge it has and understand the processes that created valuable knowledge. Group conferencing plays a particularly important role in agile knowledge management. Used correctly, group conferencing can create and capture knowledge not only for immediate application by the people that created it, but also for later reuse (in hyperlinked form) by others. Intranets play an important role not only in hosting group conferences, but also in making knowledge webs available across the enterprise.

Agile
Operations

This part hits at the heart of agility: agile operations. Here is where the engines of agility create value. We begin with an examination of agile teaming, a phenomenon related to virtual teaming, but designed to *operate agilely*. We take a lifecycle approach to agile teaming, showing how from design to dissolution, teaming policies, protocols and performance are dictated by agile principles.

In the middle two chapters of this part we turn to key services in the agile enterprise: learning and law. These may seem an unusual set to focus on. But the importance of these disciplines to agility, and the implications of networking for the future of learning and law make them essential topics.

Agile management is critical to the success of agile enterprises and is not yet well understood. In Chapter 13 we try to use "Occam's Razor" to peel away some of the complexities of management and focus on those attributes and practices that help sustain the effectiveness of agile people, processes and technologies.

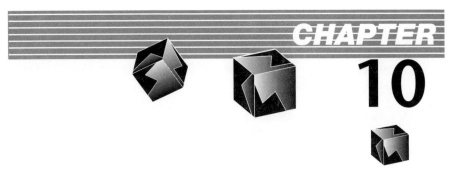

AGILE TEAMING

Agile teams are the instruments of agile networking; they do the work of agility. Ultimately, they provide the customer solutions, leverage resources, master change, and compete through cooperation. That is, they create value for customers within the framework of the principles of agility.

Agile teaming is a variety of virtual teaming, a practice that is enjoying widespread application and even more diverse definition. (Indeed, the essence of virtual teaming is "cooperating to compete.") In this chapter we'll define agile teaming, contrasting it with the more familiar virtual teaming, and we'll illustrate the benefits of agile through three examples.

1. *Product and service development teams:* We'll focus on a common element of product development cycles: specification changes.

2. *Program teams:* Agile program teams differ from project teams in that their work is less focused on a single deliverable, runs a longer term, and can experience more change in purpose (for example, spinning off subprojects or tasks). Our discussion focuses on the best practices networks used by groups across industry and in an educational institution.

3. *Product support teams:* The focus here is on sales support teams, specifically, how a worldwide sales organization uses agile networking to compete in its fast-changing environment.

This is not the place to present a history of teams and teaming, but we do want to define agile teaming in part by contrasting it with earlier, more familiar forms. First we'll spend a moment on virtual teams.

Virtual Teaming

What Virtual Teaming Isn't

Virtual teams are hot. More and more people we ask tell us that indeed they are part of virtual teams and have been so for some years (this generally prefaces the rebuttal of an offer of help). Indeed, we've been told by team members that their teams are virtual because at least one of the following is true:

- They use email.
- They have a web site.
- They work in different buildings.
- They use PCs.
- They live in different countries.
- They work at home.
- They use cell phones.
- They have movable office partition walls.
- They live in different cities.
- They collaborate.

These may all be attributes of specific virtual teams, but they don't get to the heart of the phenomenon. Nor do they explain how the term virtual became associated with this kind of teaming.

Why "Virtual" Teams?

Virtual, as in virtual team or virtual organization, is understood in the sense of "something that appears to be what it isn't." Most obviously, a virtual organization isn't really "an" organization but a group of members from different organizations, appearing, because of their focus, as one. Likewise, a virtual team isn't a team in the sense of a permanent working group. It is an aggregation of people from different organizations working together temporarily with a unified purpose.

But there is a second linguistic thread to consider here; virtual has been used in conjunction with virtual memory. *Virtual memory* is computer memory that apparently exists in RAM, but is really no more than a clever addressing scheme that fools the computer. Memory appears to be there but isn't. This connection to electronics has brought the connotation of "using computers" to virtual teams. Actually, most virtual teams do use computers and telecommunications to do their work.

What Virtual Teaming Is

Virtual teaming[1] is purpose driven, collaborative knowledge work. It involves stakeholders from a variety of organizations, usually in a variety of locations. Virtual team members' primary tools are information systems and communications networks. Membership is determined by having a needed competency, not by organizational allegiance or position in a hierarchy. Virtual teams are not permanent: when the purpose disappears, the team disappears.

Virtual teams design aircraft, perform surgical procedures, teach courses, consult, negotiate contracts, and track hurricanes. They often work as virtual teams without even thinking about it. But the advantage of thinking about it is that there is a growing canon of experientially based virtual teaming lore that can help teams to overcome the many barriers to higher-performance virtual teaming.

Benefits of Virtual Teaming

Benefits of virtual teaming include the following.

- Recruiting the best competencies available, not just those in the organization or the neighborhood
- Dealing effectively with the realities of today's work: time compression, distributed resources, increasing dependency on knowledge-based input, the need for flexibility and adaptability, and that most of the information we use today is in electronic form

---

1. We like to use the word teaming, instead of teams, in order to emphasize that the work defines the team, not the reverse.

- Taking advantage of the electronic infrastructure, enabling teams to
  - Work in parallel rather than serially
  - Have continuous access to the latest and best knowledge and information
  - Participate from their home sites, without abandoning other threads in their multiplexed work and home lives
  - Bring new team members up to speed through the on-line record of the ongoing work
  - Capture their learning electronically and make it easy for other teams to access this learning, often in real time

Virtual Teams and Traditional Teams

Virtual teams did not suddenly spring into view. They evolved from distributed teams, an artifact of the 1980s. Distributed teams usually grew up in organizations that fostered teaming across geographically distributed functions, but performed traditional work at the traditional pace.

Table 10–1 summarizes some differences between traditional and virtual teams.

Table 10–1 Traditional versus Virtual Teams.

Traditional Teams	Virtual Teams
Membership from same organization	Members from different organizations
Members trained and often certified against established standards	Members selected because of demonstrated competence
Roles and expectations per job title	Expected to perform by situation
Hope for trust	Require trust
Work processes rigid and defined	Work processes flexible and adaptive
Position authority	Knowledge authority
Persuade through power	Persuade through influence
Assert one's perspective	Negotiate, make trade-offs
Stable work environment	Environment continuously changes
Formal communications minimized	Continuous structured communications
Members work together	Members work together apart
Hierarchical	Hierarchical and networked

As we can see, virtual teaming placed a new set of values on traditional teaming. The new message was that the environment (that is, markets and competition) demanded economically produced, high-quality products in much shorter time frames, challenges that could be met only through competency-based work. Traditionally, this would mean scouring the organization for the needed competencies; even commodity-level capability would do. Going outside was a last resort. Now virtual teams start off by looking for the best competencies, wherever they may reside, in the knowledge that these competencies are available through the network. As a result, these teams can meet the most challenging market demands.

Agile Teaming

Agile teaming is a natural refinement of virtual teaming, citing the capability to react quickly to change as the highest virtue. Virtual teams implicitly embody the agile principles of cooperating to compete and leveraging resources. Agile teams go further, explicitly reflecting agile considerations in their formation and operation. We define agile teams as virtual teams that are explicitly

- Created to meet challenges requiring agility (for example, rapid response to niche opportunities)
- Designed with collaborative, agile processes in mind (for example, scanning the environment, flexibility, continuous learning)
- Operated in accordance with agility principles (especially cooperate to compete)
- Quickly formed and just as quickly disbanded when an initiative ends (for example, the creation and deletion domain discussed in Chapter 5)
- Networked: supported by networking processes and technologies

We include the last item in the definition for emphasis: virtual teams and agile teams are usually networked; if they are not, they will suffer.

The Agile Teaming Life Cycle

Like virtual teams, agile teams don't form naturally; they must be convened, designed, operated, and supported. Agile networking concepts, processes, and tools are instrumental at each of these life-cycle phases and will provide the focus here, as indicated in the following sections.

Convening an Agile Team

Strategic Alignment, Not Skunkworks

As suggested earlier, agility is not a tactic nor a point solution to a competitive threat. To have predictable start-up times, access to the best competencies, robust networking technologies, and reliable support, the charge of agile teams must be aligned with the organization's strategic direction.

This is not to say that ad hoc agile teams cannot succeed. Indeed, there is much evidence to the contrary. For example, products that emerge from "skunkworks" operations, such as those made famous at Lockheed Martin and IBM, are often the result of agile teamwork.

But the very fact that clandestine projects were required to get important work done reflects on the organization's overall lack of agility.

In order to create a product in response to market changes, organizational processes had to be circumvented. In isolated instances such stratagems work, but today's unforgiving environment requires that agility be a mainstream, not an outlaw capability.

Advice to teams: Agile teaming must be strategically aligned.

Competency Based, Including Agility Competency

Having a purpose in mind for the agile team is a first step. Next the sponsoring organization must identify the competencies that the team will need to get its work done. These competencies go beyond the expertise that maps to project needs. Because speed and response to change are paramount to agility, team members and their home enterprises must exhibit flexibility at all levels, ranging from legal agreements, to decision making processes, to personal preferences. The best graphic designer in the world, if she refuses to accept market-driven changes, will be a detriment to an agile team.

Advice to teams: Agility is a personal competency.

Writing the Contracts

In Chapter 14 we discuss some of the legal issues that arise in trying to operate agilely across corporate and organizational borders. In the best of all possible worlds, the team's mission itself would be of such power that trust and responsibility would engulf members, with no need for legal scaffolding. However, this doesn't happen even in the most holy of missions.

Wars drag on because allies quibble over turf, and critical medical research is stymied by refusals to share data. So trust and goodwill must be contractually shored up. But, as we will see, there is legal agility. Safeguards on risk, intellectual property, and profit can be built in minimal time with maximum flexibility. In agile environments the risk to competitiveness of legal delays can far outweigh the risk to profits from fast engagement.

Advice to teams: Keep legal contracts to a minimum, but flexible. Use fixed-period memoranda of understanding across teaming partners. Have agile processes in place to change agreements as conditions change.

Designing Agile Teams

Launch the Team

Having identified a strategic need for an agile team and the competencies required for its work, the next step is a kickoff or launch meeting. There is nothing new here; all teams have launches. Some teams even have virtual launches, in which members hold their first meeting electronically. We don't recommend this; every virtual or agile team should get together at least once during their tenure and preferably at the beginning. However, our purpose here is not to discuss kickoff meetings, but to point to specific agile concerns that need to be addressed in such meetings.

The primary focus of the agile launch is twofold:

1. To assure that an agile mental model exists in team members' minds
2. To design processes that will support agility.

Here is where agility as a personal competency first comes into play. Agile teams design themselves; they construct their own agile policies and processes to align with strategic goals. This is not an option but a necessity for agility. Unless teams themselves design the policies and processes by which they work, they will be unable to change them in response to new circumstances. They will not know the underlying assumptions and intentions of existing policies and processes, which will make changing them a highly risky business.

Agile Teams Design Themselves on Agile Networking Principles

Briefly put, agile teams design themselves like the networks that support them, as discussed in Chapter 6.

1. Purposes are established.
2. Competencies (or nodes) are identified.
3. Relationships (or links) are established between the nodes.
4. Switching processes are implemented to facilitate and manage change in both the nature of links and the nodes being connected when purpose changes.

To cite a simple example, an international agile team convenes to publish a catalog of new automobile specifications for the coming year. The key nodes include the following:

- Manufacturers (source information)
- Dealers and customers (the market and its requirements)
- Book design (product specification document)
- Research (competency A)
- Technical writing (competency B)
- Illustration (competency C)
- Editing and production (competency D)
- Distribution (competency E)
- Manufacturer's specs (source information)
- Book drafts (product)
- Store and direct mail houses (product delivery system)

Any *virtual team* would connect these nodes with a network to support information flow and the continuous open communication essential to build and sustain trust. An *agile team* goes beyond this to ensure that the forces of change will not thwart the team's work. Examples of this designed-in agility could include the following:

- A policy to use the lowest common denominator communications to ensure that all team members can participate fully in the information stream.
- Decision-making processes that are created specifically by and for the team, together with agreed methods for changing these processes.

- A plan that specifies protocols for using communications in a variety of circumstances. Such a plan is developed and agreed to by team members. It provides guidelines for titling messages, check-in and response times to various kinds of communication and for determining thresholds for change orders. For example, does a 10,000 Lira change in the price of a Maserati qualify as a change?
- Clearly defined and documented network-based concurrent work processes. These bring research, writing, design, and editing into parallel; no one function operates for an extended period without interaction with other functions. These microperiods of work ensure that change, or the need for change, will not go unnoticed by any function.
- Defined roles for team members. These address the needs of a team and its members, faced with large amounts of rapidly changing data. It includes roles for knowledge managers, communications managers, and leaders who understand the stress caused by such work. And, these roles themselves often shift during the life of the team.
- Processes designed to facilitate revision as well as creation. The best examples of this are today's ubiquitous word-processing programs. These recognize that a writer's greatest need is not to input, but to revise, and reflect this need in the preponderance of available functions.
- Policies to ensure that all documents, including the product document, are written, circulated, revised, edited, reviewed, and archived in electronic form until final production.
- Consideration of alternative means of publishing: the web in addition to paper catalogs.
- Learning capabilities built into the work system. These can be expert-led on-line conferences on new safety regulations and technologies; access to web sites describing new materials, or audioconferences to share late-breaking news.
- A reward system based on sharing information and knowledge

What's as important as the design of their roles, processes, and infrastructure is the built-in capability for redesign, for adaptation to change. In agile work, you don't go by the book; the book reflects what you've got to accomplish today.

Agile Teaming Performance

Just as agile teams are self-designing, they are self-operating. Leadership can provide direction in areas of specific competency, but things happen too fast for any command and control to be effective. This is not to say that there is no management interest in what's going on, but the team must be entrusted with its own operational destiny.

And this makes perfect sense, given the care taken to establish flexible processes at the outset. With the team having networked instantaneous access to information, ubiquitous peer-to-peer communications, voluntary knowledge sharing, and visible goals and expectations, there's not much for management to do but provide leadership and resources and measure what's happened in terms of the agile change domains. In Chapter 13 we'll deal specifically with what management can do to support and keep up with the work of agile teams. Perhaps the best way to look at the operational stage of agile teams is to look at a few examples.

Agile Product Development Teams

It is a commonplace that two of the greatest barriers to getting any project finished on time are change and communication about change. Every business plan looks good until tested against the realities of real work. The reason why many projects fail to deliver on promise is underestimation of the impact of change. The magnitude of these problems, even in traditional projects such as building skyscrapers or new commercial aircraft, has stimulated the development of very formal *change order* processes. Every product development team should have processes that set expectations for and facilitate the communications required to understand the following:

- Need for a change
- Implications of making or not making the change
- Effects of proposed changes on other aspects of the work

Agile teams carry such change processes to further levels. They build in ways to modify the change processes to meet unique circumstances. They can do this because of their communication and knowledge-sharing networks. Also, they make sure that they learn from the change and its effects to be better prepared next time. And there will be a next time.

Engineering Change Orders

Consider this example. A major aerospace contractor was under pressure from the U.S. government to drive cost overruns out of an ongoing missile program. It made the strategic decision to make change control the focus for breakthrough improvement.

This contractor's work is performed by teams made up of design engineers, suppliers of materials, customers for the finished product, and manufacturing process people. The specific organizational process chosen as the focus for agility was the Engineering Change Order (ECO). This is the process that manages significant changes to key documents relating to the complex system (that is, product) being built. The ECO process includes a range of activities, ranging from detecting the need for a change, dissemination of the information describing the change, negotiation support for weighing alternative solutions, and finally to formal decision.

The ECO process has all the hallmarks of a good candidate for agile design. It is

- change-related,
- time sensitive,
- information and communication intensive, and extremely complex,
- requires participation from the entire team.

To create their agile ECO process, the team first modeled and simulated the process as traditionally performed, learning where the real drivers of time and cost lay. Then, using this information as a reference point, they conceptualized a new process, based on the available network infrastructure, that would ensure the quality of changes while compressing the time it took to make them. Figure 10–1 illustrates this initial model.

By contrast, as shown in Figure 10–2, the agile ECO model uses the networking infrastructure and the team's agile networking capabilities not only to neutralize the time and cost drivers, but to build further agility. Thus, the team created a process that not only contributed to the agility of the product development initiative, but in itself was agile in that it could be easily modified according to circumstances.

The agile ECO process proceeded as a flexible, parallel activity, because the network provided the links between people, their knowledge, and the information that they needed on a continuous basis.

- Email distribution lists were prepared for use when announcing the need for an engineering change and when convening the review process. All milestones in the review process were announced through email.
- Expertly facilitated intranet group conferences were automatically created to sustain dialogue for each change proposal. Threads in each conference were dedicated to
    - Publishing the relevant documents, including situation descriptions, proposed changes, standards and so forth
    - Dialogue about defects and problems, as well as proposed changes
    - Recommendations and concerns from stakeholders affected by the proposed changes
    - Posting of decisions
- Professionally facilitated audioconferences were arranged for real time, voice resolution of specific issues. The minutes of these conferences were placed in the appropriate group conference thread.
- A videoconference was arranged for the approval and signoff session.

The advantages of such an agile process included the following:

- Dramatic reduction in time. Through accelerated information preparation, continuous dialogue, constant availability of all documentation, and elimination of travel to meetings and meetings themselves, time formerly consumed in routine activity was dedicated to value-adding work.

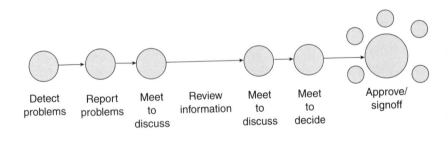

| Detect problems | Report problems | Meet to discuss | Review information | Meet to discuss | Meet to decide | Approve/ signoff |

Figure 10–1 Traditional Engineering Change Order Model Showing Serial Time-Consuming Steps.

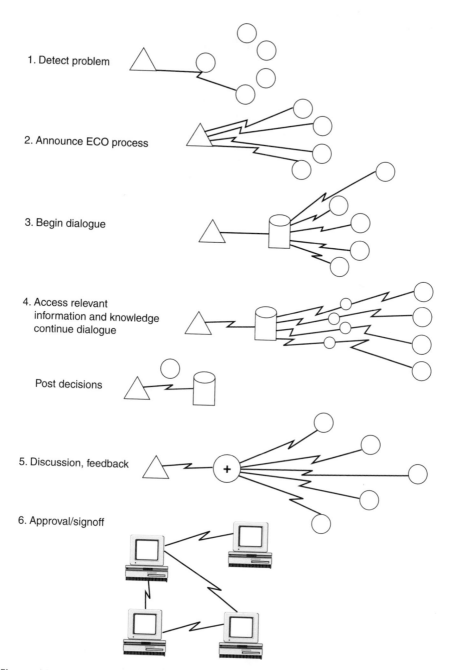

1. Detect problem

2. Announce ECO process

3. Begin dialogue

4. Access relevant
information and knowledge
continue dialogue

Post decisions

5. Discussion, feedback

6. Approval/signoff

Figure 10–2 Agile Engineering Change Order Model Showing Concurrent Time-Compressing Activities.

- Increase in the quality of decisions. With all stakeholders having open access to documents and input to the dialogue, problems and solutions were better understood and less likely to cause later problems.
- Continuous dialogue among stakeholders created a beneficial phenomenon called "the phantom reviewer." This was a personification of the collaborative viewpoint, different from any single person's, that arose from the group's interaction.
- Reduction in costs. Wasted time and poor quality are major cost drivers. Accelerating the process and delivering right decisions saved both immediate and downstream resources.

Speeding up Approval Processes

Our example has highlighted just one aspect of agile product development. Often gains can be made by applying agile networking principles to fairly routine tasks. For example, the manager of a U.S. military fast prototyping shop decided that a major barrier to his distributed prototyping team's taking on new, niche work was the time consumed in gaining all the approvals required to purchase raw materials.

Opportunities came quickly at any one of three sites spread across a wide geography. Often a customer on the shop floor would mention his need to an operator working on a current order. The request would first be passed on to the scheduler, who held a morning-long weekly meeting to match demand to capacity. After a project was accepted, the long process of up-the-line approval for purchasing materials and tooling would begin. By the time the bureaucracy got through with the purchase order, often the customer had tired of the wait and turned to a private manufacturer.

The manager of the group addressed the problem in the following ways:

- Cross-training everyone to understand the capabilities of other shop functions besides their own. This ensured that operators of various precision machines knew not only their own capabilities, but the overall capabilities of the group.
- Training the group to realize that the customer is an equal member of the team and that everyone in the group is a salesperson.
- Empowering senior people on the shop floor to evaluate and take on potential work directly from customers.

- Finding the technology driver in the group and establishing him or her as the "communications wizard" who would build:

    - A web page to market their wares

    - An email system to connect everyone in all three groups with each other and potential customers

    - An on-line scheduling database accessible by everyone in the group

- Gaining blanket purchase order approval for operators. Any senior operator had approval to make on the spot purchasing decisions for up to $25,000.

The new scenario for taking on a niche project goes as follows: A customer needing rapid prototyping makes first contact in person or through the group's web page. This gives a rich account of the group's capabilities and graphically presents examples of their work. The customer indicates a need to someone in the group, either by email or phone or through a question to an operator on the floor. The operator knows the group's capabilities and can access the on-line scheduling base. Therefore, he or she can provide immediate answers on when the job can be undertaken and the investment outlay needed. An email exchange with the scheduler formalizes acceptance and in many cases work begins immediately.

At the time of this writing, the new agile process has provided a substantial increase in orders and negligible abuse of new guidelines. An interesting by-product of the agile process is that the dreaded 4-hour scheduling meetings have all but disappeared. They have been replaced by a 5- to 10-minute daily check-in, soon to be replaced by an asynchronous on-line group conference.

Agile Program Teams

It's useful to distinguish between agile teams, such as those described, who are focused on near-term projects, and agile programs that have a more extended life cycle. These programs are often set up for continuing initiatives, such as systemic total quality, diversity, and customer satisfaction. Here we will use as an example a kind of program that is growing in popularity in all kinds of enterprise: *best practices networks*.

It's no mystery why enterprises should be interested in best practices. In times of rapid change, increasing complexity, and short times to market, it behooves an organization to understand, gather, and make the best of its knowledge. Best practices are the process corollary of people competencies. They describe ways of doing things that have given good results. They save the time normally consumed in reinventing work.

It's not difficult to see how best practices networking fits into the canon of agile networking.

- Rapid access to the best concepts, processes, and knowledge helps create solutions that enrich the customer.
- It entails mastering change by capturing and making available existing knowledge for application to sudden new circumstances.
- The process itself leverages resources (knowledge and networks) in the enterprise. Best practices networks can be thought of as a particular design of knowledge management.
- It entails cooperation between contributors and new users of that knowledge.

One particular implementation of a policy for best practices is *best agile networking practices*. These are a set of capabilities that return agile benefits and more often than not involve networking. The distinction is important. The example we will look at here is of a best practice network that we believe in itself is a best agile networking practice.

The example itself is a type, rather than an instance; the attributes we describe are real, but we have seen it implemented with minor changes in three entirely different environments: the energy industry, high tech, and higher education. Again, keep in mind that in this case the best practices network is an example of a best agile networking practice, while the best practices collected in the network may or may not be agile.

In these two cases, the best practices network was a top-down initiative fully aligned with and supported by corporate leadership. The decision to have such a network was based on several assumptions.

- There was no time for every individual part of the organization to invent its own best practices.
- Access to finalized best practices could be made available to everyone through the corporate intranet.

- Given the rate of change, best practices was to be an ongoing initiative for which change in the knowledge base was as important as creation.
- Best practices were a prime example of a reusable corporate asset.
- Best practices from outside the enterprise were as valuable as those internally generated.
- Bringing the best practices model into the corporation would stimulate collaboration across previously stovepiped organizations.

What was particularly striking was that while each of these corporations represented different industries, had different cultures, and utilized different networking technologies, all shared these assumptions!

The Energy Company

The first case is an energy company with a strong history of stovepiped organizations distributed around the world. It implemented group conferencing networks to support a best practices database and the dialogue about the knowledge captured therein. The key to the success of these networks was the integration of people, knowledge, communication, and tools. Several design points stand out.

- A corporate-wide training program was created to introduce the mental model of the best practices approach.
- Each area of expertise (fuels, chemicals, and refining) built its own databases, following knowledge management and intranet publishing procedures like those outlined in Part 2. Then the people who facilitated these databases formed their own networks, which in turn linked to executive management.
- Key practitioners were identified for every best practice who would help integrate the best practice into each area of the company's business.
- The company made a major investment in the facilitation of the network. Leaders from all sectors of the company were motivated, trained, goaled, and supported in the role of managing a network of contributors who sought out best practices in their areas of expertise.
- Network facilitators had their own group conferences in which they could share best practices in the collection of best practices.
- Network facilitators emphasized the importance of continuous communication about best practices through the group conferences.

- Specific templates were created for the collection, discussion, and implementation of best practices. Each facilitator was trained in applying these templates and could dialogue with other facilitators about their experience of applying them.
- A direct incentive was provided through a policy of measuring work team productivity against key performance indicators for every best practice. Many of these indicators represented agile capabilities, like time to respond to niche orders from valued customers or ability to reconfigure processes. What these indicators measured was organizational value—remember in Chapter 9, we said that all knowledge management initiatives need to demonstrate their bottom-line value.

Because of the predictable design of the system and specific templates employed, the best practices from anywhere in the company were accessible anywhere in the company.

The Virtual University
With some modifications this same kind of best practices program, involving collaboration across functions, has been put in place by different kinds of enterprises, including universities.

However, in reality, collaboration is not a hallmark of university life. Students are usually punished for collaborating. Faculty are often dissuaded from collaborating for fear of losing the knowledge edge that gives them value. Nor is agility a word that leaps to mind when discussing academia. One dean recently told us of a department's specific policy to institute "inertial processes." These processes were carefully designed to resist changes in educational practice, which they dismissed as learning fads.

Best practices programs are most readily adopted, however, when they are outside existing turf wars. Where we have seen a best practice network work well in education is in the development of a new form of educational establishment, the virtual university.

One of the challenges facing public universities around the world is providing access to continuous, lifelong learning to students. With the limitations of campus space, distances of people from centers of learning, and the large percentage of full-time working students, the answer seems to be in distance, or virtual, learning. We will look closely at agile learning in Chapter 11 and agile education in Chapter 16. Here we want to look briefly at how emerging virtual universities are using the best practices networks.

In the 23 campuses of the California State University system (CSU), there is debate about how to meet the needs of the university's stakeholders—learners in California. These are lifelong learners, predominately adults who work, not the "traditional" 18- to 21-year-old on-campus student. Given tight budgets, expected increases in enrollments, distances from campuses in rural areas, and the environmental impact of "windshield time" on the freeways, the CSU Chancellor's Office has sponsored an investigation of virtual learning. Given that university students and faculty are major users of the Internet, it comes as no surprise that the academy would be leading the way in web work and associated innovations.

CSU is taking the an agile route to a virtual university (in fact, as Chapter 16 explains, it's sensibly using a different name for this initiative, but virtual university will do for now). It is looking at capabilities, rather than organization. It does not want to create another bureaucracy that could become a barrier to campuses wishing to provide just-in-time learning for fast-emerging niche markets. The vision is to build a network that would enable campuses to have access to system-level services, perhaps such as marketing, while retaining full sovereignty over their best competency: the ability to supply learning. The entire system would function as an agile team network, with the nodes networked into the system and contributing their unique competencies to the system goal of providing learning to customers.

CSU established a small working team to flesh out this vision into implementable processes and designs for a possible virtual university. The inquiry began by establishing a web site and listserver on the system's intranet: this was their workplace.

One of the first items of business was to begin collecting best practices from campuses in the CSU system and around the world. The purpose of the best practices collection was to provide guidelines to the campuses for ways in which to provide virtual learning. This included not only pedagogies for the different distance learning technologies, but student support, administrative processes, marketing, recruiting, and all other processes involved in the life cycle of a learner's relationship with a university campus.

To this end, stakeholders from all CSU system campuses throughout the 1,000 mile length of California were invited to contribute what they considered to be examples of best practices in virtual education. A remote resource in Europe collected candidate best practices examples for virtual education practice across the world. All best practices were shared on the network and decisions made as to the relevance and impact of each, leading to definition of best practices for the CSU itself.

We'll look at the CSU initiative in more detail in Chapter 16. The point here is just to emphasize that all the enterprise can help to build agility by using the artifact of a best practices network. The technology is ubiquitous and the support knowledge is available; what's required is the vision and the will.

Agile Product Support Teams

Support areas in which agile teaming perspectives and practices can return significant benefits include marketing, training, and sales support. Here we'll cite a brief example of sales support teaming. As manager of sales and support administration for the Americas Geography, Bill Olson of Hewlett–Packard leads a cast of thousands that's charged with providing support for sales worldwide, where and when it's needed. Bill had seen the centrally located sales support teams languish. They were out of touch with what was going on at the front lines and didn't seem to be able to anticipate or even respond to sales' need for information and contract support.

A particular challenge was the negotiations support group. These were individuals spread all over the world who helped salespeople deal with the fine contractual issues that need to be mutually satisfied before a deal is closed. Negotiations support had always been stovepiped. People were assigned to specific industries and there was little of the knowledge sharing so central to leveraging knowledge assets to sustain agility. Olson changed that by addressing the usual suspects—people, process, and technology—in terms of agility.

Bill set up a small team that set out to understand the principles of agile learning and train the group in virtual thinking. Charged to set up learning networks, his direct reports very quickly developed an architecture and process model of *nested* networking, implemented in group conferencing on the corporate intranet. The learning networks enabled negotiators to share their knowledge with each other, making it possible to address new situations with experiential knowledge. Managers began goaling people not only as individual contributors, but as part of a team. They were measured on how much they contributed knowledge and how much they influenced others to contribute and to take up the knowledge offered.

The transformation took place within just a few months, and both direct and indirect benefits are already clear. Problem solving is now a continuous process, not a periodic crisis. People are becoming more comfortable with virtual work, and the requirement for periodic meetings is diminishing rapidly.

Dissolving Agile Teams

We remember from the discussion of change domains in Chapters 5 and 6 that a key measurement of agility is not only the ability to create, but to delete. The shorter the duration between full engagement in one project and entry into another, the more satisfactory to both employees and manager. Nothing good happens in this period. At one time a gradual "ramping down" was considered important; people could catch their breath and review the project learnings: the dreadful post-mortem that never provided much learning at all. With real-time networked access to the team's documents and dialogue and the electronic record captured in the network, such post-mortems are largely unnecessary. More valuable is on-line discussion about what happened, what worked and didn't work, and ultimate capture of project best practices and a contribution to the agile knowledge management we described in Chapter 9.

When an agile team finishes its tasks, the team should be dissolved immediately. What follows for the members could be either R&R or a new engagement, depending on the stresses of the past project. With team members sure of their competencies and available as virtual team members anywhere, they can quickly begin creating value elsewhere. Organizations can help this transition by providing an on-line database of current needs accessible to everyone through the corporate intranet. In short, when it's over, it's over. A short, social, celebratory meeting, on-line or face-to-face, is all that's required.

Summary

Agile teams are the key instruments of agile networking. Like virtual teams, they are purpose driven and competency based, they do collaborative work, and the members are from different organizations and usually different locations. Their primary tools are networked information and communication systems. But additionally to virtual teams, agile teams are created to meet challenges requiring agility, are designed to respond to change, and are quickly formed and disbanded.

Agile teams have a life cycle. They need to be convened (rather than tolerated) with strategic goals, by people who have mastered agility, with flexible contractual arrangements. They design themselves through continuous switching of tasks, competencies, and connections as situations require, based on an understanding that change to their composition, goals, and processes is inevitable. Agile teams perform a variety of tasks and typically redesign existing processes to exploit the networked agile environment. Finally, agile teams dissolve, leaving behind a record of the work that they did to be transformed into best practices for the enterprise.

AGILE LEARNING SERVICES

In the Industrial Age, we go to school;
In the Communication Age, schools come to us.

Masthead of *The Online Journal of Distance Education*

Here we describe how the agile enterprise uses networking tools to support enterprise-wide learning. We derive requirements for an agile learning service, which facilitates the acquisition of knowledge in the agile enterprise. We outline how this would work, embracing not only formal course delivery, but also informal learning in the workplace. What we present is probably a dramatic departure from the technologies and style of operation of existing training departments.[1] We shall, however, show that through adopting agile principles a training department can become a valued partner in the business of the agile enterprise.

1. We'll use the terms "training department" or "training center" to refer to those parts of an organization that traditionally provide learning opportunities and events to the work force. While we may be accused of prejoratively using an old-fashioned term, it is at least a term that everyone understands.

This topic follows on well from Chapter 9 on knowledge management. One of the issues about knowledge management hinted at there, but not discussed fully, is how the agile enterprise as a whole acquires knowledge—or learns. We showed how the process of valuing knowledge leads naturally to asking how we embed that knowledge in the right people.

We also talked about utilizing knowledge. That is, having delivered the right knowledge at the right time to the people who need it, it is up to them to utilize it. Utilizing knowledge entails learning, and it also enhances learning. Hence knowledge management creates the backdrop for learning in the agile enterprise. As we shall see, this learning is often informal—learning that is not signposted or necessarily recognized, but takes place nonetheless.

Knowledge management also teaches us some important aspects of formal learning. The authors referred to in Chapter 9, Manville and Foote,[2] note that "knowledge pull" by communities of practice has implications for learning (knowledge acquisition) strategies. People in communities of practice need to acquire knowledge *when* they need to acquire it. This means emphasis on just-in-time learning strategies, where learning is delivered to people when they need it and where they need it. We shall see here how the agile enterprise can recruit network tools to provide just-in-time formal learning.

In this chapter, we explore learning in the context of an agile enterprise in the commercial sector. Its main business is creating solutions for business customers or private individuals. We're not assuming that the enterprise is itself an educational organization. Certainly, much of what we say here about agile, network-based learning is relevant to an educational institution. Because agile education is an emerging and important aspect of agility, we devote Chapter 16 to describing agility in the education sector.

Relevance to Agility

The foremost reason for the agile enterprise to be concerned with learning is to support the agile principle of mastering change. In Part 1 we saw that to master change the agile enterprise needs readily reconfigurable operations. While aspects of that reconfigurability have to do with processes and infrastructure, a key element is an adaptable work force. An adaptable

2. Brook Manville and Nathaniel Foote, "Strategy As If Knowledge Mattered," *Fast Company*, April/May 1996.

work force can set down old practices and learn new practices and adopt them to create a greater diversity of product—either knowledge product or physical product.

Part of creating an adaptable work force is the availability of learning opportunities. People across the enterprise need to be able to rapidly acquire the new knowledge and skills that allow them to undertake new tasks. This will happen not once in their lifetimes, but continuously, as the enterprise continually evolves to shape its products to changing customer needs and changes in the wider business environment.

The second reason for the agile enterprise to be concerned with learning has to do with knowledge management, which in turn is related to leveraging resources.

The third reason to be concerned with learning is that it is the only way in which the agile enterprise internalizes change in the external business environment, again an aspect of mastering change.

A Note about Terminology

A few words about terminology are in order. Here we're using the term *learning* for a process by which nonmaterial capability is acquired; that is, the acquisition of skills and knowledge.

Like knowledge, discussed in Chapter 9, learning is a personal transform. Courses or resources are not themselves learning. They are materials from which someone may learn. Whether someone does learn from a set of materials depends on a large number of variables. The world of education spends a lot of time studying these variables to discover how people learn best.

Training is often used synonymously with learning. However, training has important overtones of practice. Training is usually more applicable to the acquisition of perceptual–motor skills. However, not all training is about perceptual–motor skills. One could be trained a cognitive skill, which could be practiced. In this case, the distinction between learning and training blurs.

We use the word *education* for the business that provides learning or training opportunities.

Introduction to an Agile Learning Service

A powerful way to consider what an agile learning service might look like is to regard an agile enterprise as the customer for its own learning services. (*Learning services* is the generic term we shall use for the arrangements by which learning is provided.) The whole agile enterprise faces directly into the challenge of meeting customer requirements in a turbulent business environment. It needs its learning services to contribute to the utmost. In fact, the agile enterprise needs its learning services to be agile. We can derive high-level requirements for an agile learning service by considering the four cardinal principles of agility.

Agile learning services enrich the customer. They are customer (learner) focused, rather than supplier (training department) focused, as follows:

- The value of a learning event is measured by the value delivered. Evaluation schemes directly measure impact on the learner's performance at his or her job.[3]
- Learning is delivered where it is needed by the customer (at the learner's workplace or home), rather than where it is convenient for the supplier (at the training center).
- Learning is delivered when it is needed by the customer (just-in-time learning, anytime learning), rather than when it is convenient to the supplier (according to a training schedule).
- Learning finishes when the learner has learned, not when the allotted course time has run out.

Agile learning services master change by delivering content that is needed by the enterprise as it evolves. Because customer requirements and the business environment change rapidly, the knowledge that people need changes rapidly, and thus learning materials that provide that knowledge must be readily adaptable and updatable.

---

3. Evaluating the impact of learning on performance is known as results-based evaluation in the influential scheme of learning evaluation defined by D. L. Kirkpatrick in 1959–1960. Results-based evaluation is the highest level of learning evaluation. Lower levels of evaluation are, in order, of behavior, learning, and reaction. A useful reference to Kirkpatrick's scheme in corporate environments is David J. Basarab, Sr., and Darrell K. Root, *The Training Evaluation Process* (Boston: Kluwer, 1992).

Agile learning services leverage resources by pulling on all the exper-tise in the enterprise to deliver learning. Providing learning is not restricted to people with "instructor" or "trainer" in their job titles. Anyone in the enterprise who has valuable knowledge to offer can do so. In this way, all the knowledge available to the enterprise is available to all the enterprise.

Agile learning services cooperate to compete by pulling in outside expertise when it is needed. The enterprise recognizes that it is unlikely to be expert in everything that it finds it needs to know in a changing business environment. It therefore actively seeks outside resources to be part of its learning system.

Hence the requirements that the agile enterprise has on its learning services are as follows:

1. Results-based evaluation
2. Learning delivered when it is needed (*anytime*[4]) and where it is needed (*anyplace*) for as long as it is needed (*self-paced*)
3. Easily adaptable courseware (*adaptable*)
4. Learning deliverable by anyone inside or outside (*anyone*)

We shall use this shopping list of requirements to assess the various learning tools available to the agile enterprise.

Requirements for Agile Learning Tools

Here we describe the principal networking tools that support learning. We restrict these to the tools that are or have been common in corporate edu-cation. We comment on how these tools support the agile learning service shopping list. All these tools allow learning to be delivered *anywhere*.

Taking a future rather than historical view, we describe these tools in the context of int*net technology.[5] Int*net technology is rapidly con-suming established learning tools and integrating them into the web environment. As we describe the int*net-based tools, we identify their nonint*net ancestors.

---

4. These single-word, italicized descriptors are used in the following to compare learning technologies.

5. As noted in Chapter 9, we are using the construction int*net to refer generically to any Internet- or intranet-based technology or system.

Electronic Mail

The simplicity of electronic mail makes it ubiquitous for communication among educators, but it is limited as an educational tool. This is because it does not have a group focus, which its cousin, computer conferencing, does. For this reason, email is hardly ever used on its own as a learning tool.

Group Conferencing

Group conferencing is any technology that allows group, text-based discussion that is time and place independent.[6] Intranet web-based discussion tools are the intranet embodiment of group conferencing; newsgroups are the Internet equivalent. The earliest form of group conferencing, computer conferencing, has been used in education for over a decade. A considerable body of expertise and experience now exists. From this we know that its principal advantages for supporting learning are as follows:

- As a group medium, it supports peer-to-peer collaborative learning. This is in contrast to the traditional model of lecture-based learning. Collaborative learning means that learners learn from interaction with each other. We say more about collaborative learning later in this chapter.
- Interaction among learners and with instructors is motivating.
- Time independence (asynchronicity) means that learning is available *anytime* and can be *self-paced*.
- Conferencing can lead to deeper-level learning than classroom lectures. Evidence is accumulating that computer conferencing classes produce higher grade scores in undergraduate education than traditional, face-to-face classes.[7]
- Because the "courseware" is highly discussion-focused, group conferencing classes are highly *adaptable*.

The principal disadvantage of computer conferencing is that using it well requires skill and time on the part of the instructor. However, almost *anyone* can contribute his or her knowledge and insights in a group conference, even if he or she cannot design and lead a class.

---

6. See Chapter 7, which describes group conferencing in more detail.

7. Jerald G. Schutte, Virtual Teaching in Higher Education (unpublished paper, Department of Sociology, California State University, Northridge, CA, 1997).

Web Pages

Intranet or Internet web pages are an emerging learning tool. They can present vast amounts of linked information. The learner can access either in-house web pages, external web pages, or a mixture of the two.

A web page can present (or give access to) text, graphics, images, animation, movies or video, and sound (including speech). Anything that can be put on a multimedia CD-ROM can in principle be delivered through an int*net web. The volume limitation of the multimedia disk is replaced by the bandwidth limitation of the connection to the int*net.

The advantages of the web-based learning tool are as follows:

- We are increasingly familiar with web-based tools and accept "the web" as a source of information.
- Web-based learning resources are under the control of the individual learner. They can learn *anytime*. They can take a *self-paced* approach and follow their own trails of interest through the linked material.
- The potential to present information in text, pictures, and sound lets web pages cater for those people who prefer to receive information verbally, visually, or auditorily.

The principal disadvantages of web-based learning resources are as follows:

- Producing high-quality web instructional material is personnel intensive and expensive. It is not a case of uploading course notes, especially if full advantage is taken of the multimedia capabilities. Creating good instructional material requires instructional and technical skills, which not everyone has. However, *anyone* can in principle provide base content to a web page, and web pages outside the enterprise can be accessed as learning resources from inside.
- The time scales and investment needed to produce good web pages often make it impossible to tailor the content for different groups of learners or to update it frequently. The content is therefore not very *adaptable*. (It is, however, more adaptable than a multimedia disk.)
- Whatever enthusiasts claim about "interactivity," the only interactivity within a web page is with the links. There is no human-to-human interactivity.

Integrated Web-based Learning Tools

As we write, a number of web-based learning tools are coming to market. These essentially combine the features of group conferencing and web pages, together with other learning management functions, into a single tool. Typical of the functions supported by these tools are the following:

- Presentation of the course schedule
- Presentation of learning materials (that is, web pages) (some tools also include special facilities for authoring educational material)
- Discussion "room" (that is, group conferencing)
- Presentation of instructor and learner profiles
- Ability to carry out assessments

Some tools also include videoconferencing and shared whiteboard applications. Through these, students and instructors can see each other and share exhibits.

Videoconferencing

Videoconferencing is increasingly used in corporate education, particularly in the plenary form whereby an instructor broadcasts to a class(es) at a distant site(s). Currently, the networks employed are in-house LANs and WANs or satellite channels. However, there are an increasing number of web-based point-to-point videoconferencing tools. It will only be time (and bandwidth expansion) before int*net provides the connectivity for at least one-way, multipoint videoconferencing. This will be particularly important for individuals' learning at their desk or home, where it may be too expensive to install high-speed networks or satellite downstations.

The advantages of videoconferencing as a learning medium are as follows:

- For an instructor, conducting a class via videoconferencing can require very little change from traditional teaching methods. Almost *anyone* can contribute to videoconference instruction, even if she or he cannot set up and lead a videoconferencing class.
- As classes are delivered live, what an instructor says is *adaptable* to the immediate learning needs. However, prepared course materials, such as integral videos and demonstrations, are less so.

- The opportunity to see and hear the instructor and peer groups, in addition to what they are presenting, is motivating. There are also opportunities for two-way communication between instructor and learners.

The disadvantages are these:

- Of all the learning technologies, videoconferencing introduces the least departure from normality. It does not introduce any rethinking of educational practice, which might open the door to an agile approach.
- Videoconference classes are not available *anytime*. Learners and instructors have to be available at the same time. Furthermore, classes are time limited, and do not allow *self-paced* learning.
- Some learners, especially managers, will only be convinced by professional-quality broadcasting, which is expensive and requires new skill sets.

Audioconferencing

Audioconferencing is the multiparty telephone conference call. It is used widely in corporate education. While currently restricted to the phone network, we can predict that int*net technologies, now capable of handling single-voice channels, will be able to support the bridged, group phone calls that audioconferencing requires.

The advantages of audioconferencing are as follows:

- Telephones are everywhere, and audioconferencing bridging services are widespread.
- The technology is so easy to use that virtually *anyone* can contribute to instruction, even if she or he cannot design and lead a whole class.
- Because the class is live, content is immediately *adaptable*.

Its principal disadvantages are as follows:

- The lack of a visual or text channel. However, audioconferencing can easily be supplemented with previously distributed visual or text materials.
- Like videoconferencing, audioconferencing classes are not available *anytime* and do not permit *self-paced* learning. However, audioconferencing does provide valuable whole-group contact when mixed with asynchronous, time-independent media.
- Running an audioconference class takes facilitation skill and a well-constructed agenda.

Summary

Table 11–1 summarizes the characteristics of the principal networked learning tools from the perspective of the agile learning service requirements described earlier. We have added a final column, which rates each tool to the degree that it supports collaborative learning. We talk about collaborative learning in the following section.

Table 11–1   How the Networked Learning Tools Support Agile Learning Requirements.[a,b,c]

Tool	Anyplace	Anytime	Self-paced	Adaptable Content	Anyone Can Contribute	Supports Collaborative Learning
Group conferencing	●●●	●●●	●●●	●●●	●●●	●●●
Web pages	●●●	●●●	●●●	●	●●	
Integrated web learning tools	●●●	●●●	●●●	●●●	●●●	●●●
Video-conferencing	●●			●●	●●●	●
Audio-conferencing	●●●			●●●	●●●	●●●

a. None of these tools supports results-based evaluation.

b. Because integrated web tools essentially combine group conferencing with web pages, we have given them the best marks of either individual tool.

c. The more dots the better.

Each of the tools listed has its advantages and disadvantages. Some are visual based, some audio based, and some text based. Some are highly interactive, others less so. Some require instructors and learners to be available at the same time and do not readily accommodate self-paced learning. Others are time independent and do support self-paced learning. However, the characteristic that they have in common is that they allow the learning to come to the learner, and not the other way round. All these tools meet the agile need for learning to be delivered where the learner wants it.

Furthermore, all these tools allow, to a greater or lesser extent, anyone inside or outside the enterprise to contribute his or her knowledge.[8] This is a particular boon for recruiting knowledge and expertise, when and where it is needed, without the cost and inconvenience of travel. Instructors and experts might be on a different continent, but nonetheless their knowledge is available to learners.

Consequently, these are all tools that should be part of the armory of the agile learning service. Through careful mixing of tools and matching to content demands and learners' requirements, it is possible to create highly effective tool suites. For example, lengthy courses employing integrated web tools can be combined with audioconferences or videoconferences to let instructors and learners "meet," talk together, and exchange questions and answers in real time.

A final point. In Chapter 7 we spoke of the need for the agile enterprise to employ group conferencing to create group communication across the enterprise. In Chapter 8 we showed the benefits of publishing information on intranet webs. In Chapter 9 we showed how intranets again are important to knowledge management. We have three good reasons already for the agile enterprise to employ group conferencing and web technology. Supporting agile learning services is a fourth. The technology for agile learning is exactly that needed for agile work.

A Note on Collaborative Learning

Collaborative learning is a powerful design for learning. It's not uniquely related to agility, but an agile enterprise will need to ensure that its learning systems are as effective as possible. So we'll take a little time to describe collaborative learning here.

Starr Roxanne Hiltz, one of the first to create computer conference

---

8. Sir Douglas Hague writes for subscribers to the UK think-tank Demos about "Unipart U." This is a learning service set up inside the UK Unipart automotive supplies company. At Unipart U, any employee can be a potential teacher. Focusing on what is needed to do the job, Unipart U reckons that the best way to learn and to show that you have learned is to teach. There are no examinations: evaluation is based entirely on whether "you can do your job better." Douglas Hague, "The Firm As University," *Demos Quarterly*, Issue 8, 1996.

classrooms with Murray Turoff in the late 1970s, defines collaborative learning as follows:

> Collaborative learning is . . . a learning process that emphasizes group or cooperative efforts among faculty and students, active participation and interaction on the part of both students and instructors, and knowledge that emerges from an active dialogue among those participants sharing their ideas and information.[9]

Hiltz goes on to identify the basic value premise of collaborative learning. It is that significant learning takes place when people "actively construct" knowledge by putting new ideas into words and receiving other people's reactions to these ideas. Teachers seek this active construction, to a limited extent, when they ask students to write essays. In collaborative learning, the same active construction is stimulated through question and answer with one's peers as much as with the instructor.

Educationalists David Johnson and Roger Johnson, summarizing decades of research on cooperative learning (or collaborative learning), conclude

> While [cooperative learning] is not perfect, and is certainly not a panacea that solves all instructional problems experienced by college professors, it has been demonstrated to be superior under most conditions to competitive and individualistic learning.[10]

Collaborative learning takes place within a group and is based on communication among that group. The communication is as much between learners as between learners and the instructor (see Figure 11–1). A variety of pedagogical designs exists to create collaborative learning in school settings. For example, the instructor can ask members of the class to comment on each others' essays or create small groups to research and present papers. In the corporate setting, collaborative learning often happens without an explicit pedagogical design, because adult learners readily share experiences and question the instructor and each other.

9. Starr Roxanne Hiltz, "Collaborative Learning in a Virtual Classroom," in *Proceedings of the Conference on Computer-supported Cooperative Work 1988, Portland, Oregon* (New York: Association for Computing Machinery, Inc., 1988), pp. 282–290.

10. David Johnson and Roger Johnson, "What We Know about Cooperative Learning at the College Level," *Cooperative Learning*, 13, no. 3, 1993.

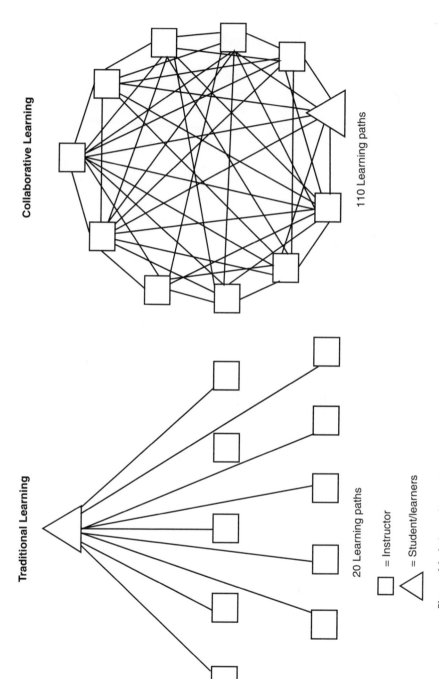

Traditional Learning

20 Learning paths

☐ = Instructor

◁ = Student/learners

Collaborative Learning

110 Learning paths

Figure 11–1 Learning Paths in Traditional and Collaborative Learning.

165

Collaborative learning is well supported by some of the networked learning tools that we reviewed previously. The test is the extent to which the tool easily allows extended interaction and communication among learners and between learners and the instructor. As Table 11–1 shows, the best tool for this is group conferencing, the worst videoconferencing, with audioconferencing in the middle.

As collaborative learning is so powerful, the agile enterprise should reengineer its learning systems on collaborative learning principles. This means, for example, that instructors become guides to knowledge and facilitators of communication, rather than sources of knowledge, a topic to which we return later in this chapter.

Informal Learning

So far, without explicitly saying so, we have been discussing an agile learning service solely in terms of its provision of formal learning opportunities. While the learning opportunity may be distributed, asynchronous, self-paced, or even entirely resource based, it is structured around courses and heavily signposted with the words "learning" or "training." It is the learning provided by training departments. The message of the previous sections was that the learning that the traditional training department offers should be looked at afresh—deconstructed and put back together again from an agile perspective using technologies and if possible employing collaborative learning designs. We might call this learning process reengineering.

However, there is another type of learning that goes on all the time in any enterprise. This is informal learning. It is learning that arises through work. It does not take place at a training center, materials don't come from a training department, and it is not labeled learning. Because it's not labeled learning with a capital L, we typically don't recognize that learning has taken place. Nonetheless, we all know that we acquire knowledge (learn) through work. We ask you to consider what you would know if all that you knew was what you had learned from formal education and training courses.

Informal learning, then, takes place at and through work and outside formal learning events. Informal learning takes place as we solve problems in our work. We overcome challenges and learn how we overcame them—be they applying a new process, using new tools, or forming different types of relationship. The sources and resources we use to solve problems and learn from are our colleagues and the knowledge in our working environment. Thus informal learning has many parallels with collaborative learning and may include collaborative learning as an informal process. Earlier we quoted Hiltz on collaborative learning. In the same article, she says that underlying the collaborative approach to learning is the principle that "knowledge is not something to be 'delivered' . . . but rather something that emerges from active dialogue among those who seek to understand and to apply concepts and techniques".[11]

Informal learning is accelerated by the networking capabilities that we have described earlier.

- *Group conferencing:* Group conferencing creates the environment for learning from one's peers through interaction with them and through exposure to material on knowledge networks. Group conferencing contributes to informal learning in three important ways.

1. It enormously widens the span of people from whom one can learn. Rather than being limited to learning from the people with whom one works day to day or can travel to meet or from the people who have found time to put their knowledge and experiences into documents, it is possible to interact with people across the whole company.

2. The opportunity to learn is constantly available at the place of work (just-in-place). It is not necessary to make special arrangements to "get at" some knowledge—one doesn't even have to leave one's desk. People can consult a knowledge network anytime that they need to know something. If and when they get an answer through conferencing, it can be immediately applied in the work situation (just-in-time). If the answer isn't there, people can post a question. Even if an answer isn't forthcoming, a browse through a conference will often identify people who are working in a relevant area, who can be contacted directly through electronic mail or telephone.

3. When using conferencing for ad hoc inquiries, it's common for a number of people to reply to a question with different answers,

11. Hiltz, "Collaborative Learning in a Virtual Classroom."

provoking the questioner to think more clearly about his or her query. Or browsing in a conference will alert someone to something that they didn't think was a question. Conferencing, therefore, not only provides people with access to a network of knowledge and knowledgeable people, but also interactions with others through conferencing helps to develop the process of inquiry.

- *Intranet publishing:* Intranet pages don't have the interactive, communication element of group conferencing (although we argue in Chapter 8 that they should be so supplemented). Nonetheless, they are an informal learning resource. They provide information that is used in work, when it is required (just-in-time) and to the desktop (just in place), and in applying that information to work, learning occurs.

- *Knowledge management:* The same is true of knowledge management systems, discussed in Chapter 9. Knowledge is disseminated through the enterprise. It's available just-in-time and just-in-place and used in work.

These networking capabilities, therefore, create the environment for informal learning. There are a number of particular characteristics of this informal learning.[12]

- Learning is continuous, not event driven. Learning takes place all the time from the information and knowledge (and people) on the network.
- Learning and work become combined (although, as we noted previously, work is recognized, but not learning). As Grenier and Metes say, "learning becomes a partner in the work process: integrated and simultaneous with the work underway."[13]
- Learning is directed by the learner, not by the curriculum. Learners search for the information and knowledge that they need, wherever it is, to whatever detail they need. Learning at work, therefore, has the characteristic of drilling down: getting to the material that makes a

---

12. These characteristics of informal learning are taken from the description of virtual learning in Ray Grenier and George Metes, *Going Virtual* (Upper Saddle River, NJ: Prentice Hall, 1995), Chapter 18.

13. Grenier and Metes, pp. 250–251.

difference and, in every likelihood, ignoring what is encountered en route. Thus informal learning has different potentials from formal learning. In a formal learning situation, the emphasis is usually on scope and structure. People's informal learning searches out specific items without, usually, much interest in the wider picture. The two complement each other well.

Given the enormous learning potential of network capabilities—group communication, intranet-hosted web pages, or knowledge management systems—it is surprising that more enterprises do not explicitly recognize that their network is a learning tool and, as we have been saying here, recognize it as an agile learning tool.

An Agile Learning Service

Here we describe the characteristics of a truly agile learning service. We describe the arrangements by which the agile enterprise both provides formal learning and embraces informal learning in the workplace.

In respect of formal learning, we summarize the agile learning services described earlier in this chapter. In respect of informal learning, we outline later how the enterprise can recruit the skills and professionalism of its training department professionals to extend and amplify informal learning.

Perhaps we need to remind ourselves why the agile enterprise is so concerned with learning. It is because much of its business is knowledge-based, in an environment where the knowledge it must value is rapidly changing. Hence learning (the acquisition of knowledge) is central to the agile enterprise. The agile enterprise exemplifies above any other enterprise the statement that the rate at which an organization can learn may become the only sustainable source of competitive advantage.[14]

With knowledge acquisition central to the business of the agile enterprise, the role of those people who are professionals in knowledge acquisition also becomes more central. But, true to the principles of agility, an agile learning service takes enriching the customer as its key mission. It

14. In Peter Senge's *The Fifth Discipline* (New York: Doubleday/Currency, 1990), p. 349, the idea of learning capability as sustainable competitive advantage is articulated by Roy Stata, CEO of Analog Devices, Inc. However, we have also seen it attributed to Arie de Geus, one-time coordinator of group planning at Royal Dutch/Shell.

moves from being regarded as an overhead to being valued as a partner in the business. It becomes integrated fully with the enterprise's operations, helping its customers to deal with the need to learn more, better, and faster. In short, it helps people in the enterprise to get work done.

The training department transitions to an agile learning service by discarding its traditional models and adopting new ones, as shown in Table 11–2. Note how these transitions are consistent with agile principles.

Table 11–2 Transition from a Training Department to an Agile Learning Service.

From	To
Organization	
Training department	Agile learning service
Regarded as a separate function	Integrated with the work of the enterprise; a partner to work teams
Success measured on basis of internal revenue accrued ("make money")	Success measured on basis of work teams' success and their judgment of value received ("help get the work done"); potential for value pricing
Training department staff keep to the training center	Agile learning service staff (learning professionals) join (physically or through the network) work teams throughout the enterprise
Communicate with other managers through formal channels	Constant communication with and within work teams to identify their learning needs
Rarely browse enterprise-wide intranets	Always browsing enterprise-wide intranets to sense newly breaking areas of valuable knowledge
Provision of Formal Learning	
Learning services bundled into product (courses)	Learning services are solutions, in whatever form they need to take, to work teams' learning needs
Reactive stance: courses developed because they are fashionable or because there is a demand of economic order size	Proactive or concurrent stance: learning solutions identified by learning professionals before or as the work teams recognize the need for them

Table 11–2 Transition from a Training Department to an
              Agile Learning Service. *(continued)*

Courses standardized, mass produced	Learning solutions always customized to make the most difference
Long lead time to produce courses	Learning solutions created concurrently with need
Courses delivered when convenient to the training department	Learning solutions delivered just-in-time using networked learning technologies
Courses delivered where convenient to the training department	Learning solutions delivered just-in-place using networked learning technologies
Pedagogy based on the transmissive, lecture model, with tutor as expert	Pedagogy based on collaborative learning with tutor as facilitator
Embracing Informal Learning	
None: concentrate on formal learning	Add value to informal learning by adding structure and scope
None: concentrate on mass learning (classes)	Help individuals to learn through coaching

Let's look a little more at the change in style of learning delivery that we're suggesting. We described earlier in this chapter how formal learning delivery should be reconstructed around agile principles using networking tools. The role for formal learning courses still remains, especially when large numbers of staff need new skills. Formal hands-on training will still be required for teaching perceptual–motor skills. Introductory and procedural training may still be course based.

However, an agile learning service adds to formal delivery, to extend the way it helps the enterprise. It adds to it by applying the pedagogical skills of its learning professionals to informal learning by work teams. Thus it embraces and becomes part of the informal learning that goes on in the workplace.

- Learning professionals become members of work teams. As they see these teams dealing with new knowledge, they undertake research to add scope and structure to newly glimpsed concepts. They rapidly create learning solutions around them. These solutions are not formal, nor necessarily long lived. They may take the form of a series of briefings or network discussions. They may be simple open learning documents. But, however formed, they structure and present the content required by the work teams according to pedagogical principles so that the learning potential is maximized.

• They become part of informal learning communities on the network, using group conferencing to maximize the learning process. They ask questions to clarify ideas. They prompt for the topic to be elaborated. They weave together different people's perspectives, identifying commonalties and disagreements. They may even help consolidation of learning by setting up quizzes.

• Learning professionals coach individuals. They do not coach because they know more about the subject matter. They coach to help the individual to learn. They identify and work with individual's different learning styles: preference for learning through concrete experience, reflection, concepts, or experimentation. They suggest learning opportunities for these individuals. They connect with their colleagues coaching others. They stay around for the long term.

This transition will not be easy nor necessarily comfortable for a training department or its staff. However, with the rest of the enterprise going through the changes required to be agile, it is difficult to find arguments that the training department should be excused.[15] Indeed, such a transition will result in a revitalization of the training department, moving it from perhaps a marginal function to a key part of getting business done.

Furthermore, an agile learning service for internal customers will readily transfer to external customers. All the considerations of agility that we have described here apply to external customers. The agile enterprise can thus acquire an important new revenue-earning capability for providing agile learning services to its business customers.

15. Nor is it easy to find arguments that any internal function should be excused from going agile. Any function that responds to an internal inquiry with such sentiments as "that's not how we do things round here" is essentially nonagile. Its lack of agility then places a load on the rest of the enterprise. For this reason we suggest in Chapter 12 that "the legal department" should transition to "an agile law service," and in Chapter 13 we make similar comments about IT/IS departments.

Summary

The agile enterprise needs an agile learning service, itself adhering to agile principles, if it is to equip its work force with the rapidly changing knowledge that they need. An agile learning service enthusiastically recruits networking tools to bring learning to the learner where and when he or she needs it. It also uses these tools to allow anyone inside or outside the enterprise to contribute his or her knowledge. It provides learning solutions that match the work force's learning needs, rather than products that are convenient to produce. An agile learning service also recognizes the reality of informal learning in the workplace and embraces it. It deploys its learning professionals into work teams to help their members to learn and to help the work to get done. An agile learning service developed inside the enterprise can readily be directed at external customers, providing a new line of revenue-earning service.

AGILE LAW SERVICES

As we construct new, fast-moving agile networks, we need to consider the implications for traditional corporate functions. Here we'll give a perspective on new challenges facing the law function in agile enterprises. Then we'll suggest an approach to recreating the law function as an effective agile law service provider.

New Challenges for Law Services

The delivery of law services has changed little in the last 20 years. But several artifacts of 21st-century agility will have major impact on the traditional approach. We look at three of these here:

1. Contractual Agents
2. Disintermediation
3. Guaranteed Trading Transactions

Contractual Agents

In an age when speed of response is paramount, time taken to identify, negotiate, and close agreements has to be reduced by orders of magnitude: from months to days or even hours. Business will address these issues through electronic contractual agents that live on networks.

These agents are software modules preconfigured to address issues such as risk assessment and liability apportionment. They perform the basic trading functions, removing much of the routine work of lawyers and purchasing communities in assessment of value, negotiating, and agreement drafting.

Contractual agents review and determine whether a likely match is possible between trading partners. They aim to agree on as much common ground as possible, leaving only the fine details to be reviewed and negotiated by human intervention. This will be particularly effective in electronic commerce, where goods and services are sold via the Internet. For orders already being placed in this way, it is a natural step to deal with the legalities and formalities through automatic contractual agents. We've heard of one international bank currently exploring the possibility of such agents operating within its independent financial advisor network, with dramatic potential cost savings and benefits.

Disintermediation

We seem to live in an age that loathes the middle: the middle class, middle managers, middle-of-the-road politicians, all are constantly under siege. The like is true for intermediators (though not for mediators, who are in great demand to settle, you guessed it, intellectual property disputes). Because of the access to goods, services, knowledge, and ideas provided by networks, non- or low-value-adding players within value chains are rapidly disappearing. Intermediators, like travel agents or distribution centers of all kinds, are disappearing as customers go straight to the producer. Many people now go directly to the Internet not so much for shopping, but for finding the niche product they know that they want.

When we look at alliances in Chapter 14 we'll discuss aggregators. These are enterprises that create value by linking customers seamlessly to a set of competencies that were traditionally supplied by separate industry segments. In the travel industry, such aggregators combine component travel services such as transportation, lodging, entertainment, business and networking support, culture, and, yes, shopping. The travel agent, in networking terms, has links to many of the component services, but stands between the consumer and them. Our travel agent can order tickets to the opera, but won't know anything about the performers. The aggregator who has the Paris Cultural Board as a member of the agile team enables us to link through the web site directly to that information. When our needs and interests change, our links change, in real time.

Disintermediation fueled by networking technology will have a considerable impact on the law profession. It will be particularly felt by the sole law practitioner who normally advises clients on how to get through cumbersome, fragmented processes. An aggregator can offer a user-friendly, quality, low-cost offering supported by state-of-the art electronic agent technology, accessible through a network service.

As disintermediation takes hold in one part of the law services profession, it is highly likely to be extended into other specialties, for example IT licensing, intellectual property protection, and alliance agreements, with devastating consequences for existing players. The only way the profession can respond to this threat is by itself becoming more agile, potentially taking a proactive role to create aggregated solutions.

Guaranteed Trading Transactions

The pace of technology deployment and the rapid emergence of new Internet trading communities are creating the demand for a legally consistent trading environment. As we write, Internet security protocols are emerging that lower the risk that on-line trading transactions are intercepted by unauthorized third parties. The issue that has arisen in its place, however, is that of the legal framework through which trading can be successfully undertaken.

Questions that are being addressed include these:

- What is an asset for the purposes of trading electronically?
- What are the core issues in the creation, distribution, and access of information assets and corresponding payment systems on the web?
- To what extent (and how) can the access, distribution, use, and abuse of information be monitored?
- When does the issue of scalability take effect?
- To what extent does proliferation of information from various sources give rise to degradation, misuse, and a possible threat to reputation?

Since the law profession is not providing answers fast enough, proposals are emerging to package transactions within limited insurance coverages that would reduce, limit, or remove the legal consequences that flow from a single transaction. Clearly, this would only cover civil liability and be capped at a certain amount, above which normal rules (or the rules that we know at that time) apply. But imagine if it were possible to purchase guaranteed trading insurance for as little as a few cents per transaction. Would this remove, conclusively, the need for direct legal involvement?

Market impatience for progress, coupled with the ability to exploit this new entrepreneurial model, ensures that such a system will develop shortly. In doing so, it will provide legal certainty as part of the in-built rules of the game and remove the regular and direct involvement of law service providers. Organizations with a vested interest in the success of electronic trading communities are, as we write, actively considering agile alliances with law and networking experts to bring the new model about.

Creating an Agile Law Service

The basic ways in which advice on law is requested and delivered, together with the underlying concepts and assumptions, have been a robust fortress against significant, turbulent change. We can inquire why this is the case.

- While all else is changing, is it comforting to know that we have a stable law system?
- In spite of "lawyer jokes," do we subconsciously hold the law profession and system in respect and reverence?
- Despite our cynicism, do we somehow feel unable to challenge those who are the guardians and arbitrators of the law?
- And therefore do we count on drive for change to come from within the law profession and not as a result of external pressure?

There are many reasons for the conservatism of the law establishment. Nonetheless, corporate law departments (and to a lesser extent professional law firms) will need to embrace fundamental reforms in the way they work or face extinction.

In Chapter 11, we described how traditional training departments can transform themselves into an agile learning service. We said as a footnote there that it was difficult to find arguments that any internal corporate function should be excused from going agile. Here we see another internal function that needs actively to pursue the agile path.

As the tension between organizations embracing change and the onboard law community resisting it increases, more energy will be put into developing agile law capabilities. We are already seeing such capabilities emerge in the widening use of time-limited, one-page memoranda of understanding (MOUs) for alliances, sent through email, instead of lengthy, detailed, ironclad contracts, nurtured through endless meetings. Such MOUs are essentially agile. Accepting agility means we can't know the future. Situations will change, making it impossible to anticipate all possible contingencies. So don't try. These MOUs are based on agreement to proceed with what is known and to make sure that processes are in place to respond to change when it inevitably occurs.

What then are some of the other transitions lawyers can adopt to get with the agility program? First, let's take a look at the problem.

The common criticism of the legal department[1] is that it takes too long to deliver its service, especially given the short and shorter life cycles of alliances, products, and information value. But the problem cannot be laid entirely at the door of the legal department. Often the business unit needing the services fails to build the kind of relationship with the law folks that facilitates the giving and taking of advice. Furthermore, lawyers are often not invited into a situation until it is well underway. When asked for quick advice, they don't know the context or background of the issues. The irony is that lawyers are kept out of early discussions for fear that they will hold things up. So goes the catch-22.

One way to address this issue is to bring the law function into the networking community of the organization. Let them participate in on-line conferences, peruse projects on the intranet, and join videoconferences. This approach parallels that which we recommended in Chapter 11 for transitioning the training department to an agile learning service. There the essential new behavior was for training professionals—here lawyers—to join face-to-face or virtual work teams to assist in getting the job done. It

---

1. We know that referring to a legal department raises the grammatical question of which departments are operating outside the law. However, common usage encourages us occasionally to use this term.

means adopting a proactive rather than reactive stance. It means accepting that the value of the law service is determined by the customer—the work team—rather than the supplier—the legal department. This is a start, but it will take more, a formal program to build an agile law service that will support the needs of the agile enterprise.

Nine Steps as a Foundation to an Agile Law Service

The following process steps are suggested as a preliminary guide to effecting lasting change within a corporate law department.

- Step 1: Recognize the problem.
- Step 2: Engage the customers; understand and appreciate their needs.
- Step 3: Brainstorm the vision of an agile law service.
- Step 4: Identify cultural, business, and technical barriers and plan to eliminate them.
- Step 5: Let lawyers understand the wider business.
- Step 6: Review technical infrastructures; explore new technology as an aid to responsive service delivery.
- Step 7: Develop a program of regular new practice scenarios.
- Step 8: Implement a comprehensive intellectual property asset inventory.
- Step 9: Change the reward structure to reinforce new behavior.

These steps outline a generic process by which agility can be attained by a corporate legal department or an independent professional law office (although we admit that we concentrate on the former). Each implementation will be different for each enterprise based on the assessment of where they are and how far they need to move.

Step 1: Recognize the Problem

Many remain unconvinced about the prospects of threatening innovations, such as disintermediation within the law services industry. They are convinced that the need will always exist for their skills. Nothing could be further from the truth. As we have indicated, the pace of business change and the impact of networking are dictating that law service provision must radically change. Otherwise, firms will be overtaken by new virtual, network-based sources of expertise that can offer proactive advice, just in time, anywhere.

Change has already come upon the law community. This change is unsummoned and in some cases unwelcome.

- The recession of the early 1990s caused a shock wave that particularly hit in-house corporate legal departments. Many lawyers, particularly in information technology companies, lost the security of positions that they had held for many years. Organizations faced with declining profitability learned how to survive without an army of in-house lawyers, to say nothing of the vast array of external advisors.
- Within the law profession itself, there has been a drive for greater openness and access. This is particularly so in the United Kingdom. Rights of access to higher courts (once the exclusive preserve of barristers) are now available to solicitors. Greater streamlining of cases and the use of skeleton arguments is seen as one way to reduce lengthy cases and weed out weak cases that have little hope of success. The soaring costs of the UK Legal Aid bill coupled with the desire for value for money from the public purse will be a key driver for reform of the total system.

So change is in the air, and leadership needs to take advantage of this mood to drive the kinds of rethinking that will support agility. A small *agile law services cell* that understands marketplace dynamics is needed to begin a transition campaign. Its function is essentially to initiate discussion about change. Its members must realize and be able to convey the message that "things will never be the same again." They must recognize that to develop agile capabilities requires a break from the past and the need to wholeheartedly embrace an unknown, but nevertheless exciting future.

Such an agile law services cell needs to highlight the commercial reality of alternative sources of advisors who can deliver more responsively and cost effectively. Because the network is dissolving the boundaries between inside and outside the organization, internal law departments are no longer immune from external competition.[2]

This cell may also decide explicitly to educate its mainstream colleagues on agility and thus the pressures and changes that the rest of the

2. For example, a European Commission-funded telematics project, Experts Unlimited, has spawned a set of European companies that offer professional advice through premium-rate telephone lines. Legal advice is part of its portfolio.

enterprise is facing. It will take confidence and leadership on the part of this small group, but attitude and enthusiasm for the task will help them to overcome any obstacles or barriers to long-lasting change.

Step 2: Engage the Customer; Understand and Appreciate Their Needs

The relationship between an enterprise's legal department and the business units is very often similar to an elderly, loving couple. They spend hours together, holding hands, sit in front of the fire, never speaking a word. In some ways, they assume that they know what the other is thinking.

Is it the case that we have grown familiar with the service provided and have no desire to challenge this powerful function to change? The need exists for the legal department to engage the business customer in new ways—to accurately ascertain the ways in which their business goals can be met by the provision of proactive law services.

What is required is a mature assessment of four major questions:

1. Do we know how best to add value to our customers? Have we analyzed cases where we were seen to add value and cases in which we were not?

2. Are we providing solutions for our customers or simply the "product" that is convenient for us to supply? How closely are we integrated with our customers' businesses?

3. Are we ready for our value added to be measured by our customers? Indeed, do we have formal procedures to ask customers to record their satisfaction with the service we supply?

4. Are we responsive to changes in customer requirements? Even, are we proactive in advising customers of changes to law that may affect their processes or identifying their changed processes that may have legal implications?

These are good questions to put to an internal law services review body. Attitude is key here. Defensiveness or fingerpointing will destroy the basis on which the review takes place. A neutral facilitator will be very valuable in these deliberations.

Step 3: Brainstorm the Vision of an Agile Law Service

Based on the assessment reached in step 2, a wider group, including customers, needs to undertake a structured brainstorming session. One useful technique that could be used is called *idealized design*. This technique helps participants to discard assumptions, constraints, and barriers that clutter their thinking and deny them the possibility of thinking "outside the box."

Techniques like this will be helpful to create a vision of the future that everyone understands and shares. If done well and to sufficient depth, they can identify the principal capabilities that need to be developed. Again, outside facilitation is an important factor.

Step 4: Identify the Cultural, Business and Technical Barriers and Plan to Eliminate Them

Having developed an idealized vision of a new agile law service, attention passes to the barriers that currently exist to its being realized. These barriers may fall into three categories: business, cultural, and technical. Assessing each in turn will enable change managers to

- Assign priorities to each barrier
- Develop a realistic action and resource plan for eliminating or reducing them
- Acknowledge that barriers cannot be overcome but must be accommodated within the new system

This requires developing an outline route map of the transition that will be required. It will also highlight areas of training, personal development, and technical infrastructure changes that must be part of the transition.

Step 5: Let Lawyers Understand the Wider Business

Historical examples exist of senior legal counsel sitting as business staff or board members in an attempt to bridge the gap between the legal and business functions. Some worked well; others, sadly, did not.

Nonetheless, there is great value in lawyers putting aside their professional role for a period and engaging in a purely business role. This means

joining business units in managerial or even technical roles. Their engagement in the wider business operations of the enterprise will have the following benefits:

- They will develop a practical appreciation of the business issues and
  difficulties facing the agile enterprise.
- They will understand the dependency that business units have for
  timely legal advice.
- They will be able to see how and where law services add the most
  value; perhaps by identifying 80:20 rules.
- They will be able to gauge and set responsive service standards.
- They personally will acquire new skills.

Lawyers undergoing this cross-functional experience should have a
responsibility to share widely the learning and experience. Group communication networks, as described in Part 2, can play a part. For example,
lawyers working in business units can provide principal input to group
conferences for the enterprise's lawyers. In these they explain their experiences of the law services–business unit relationship.

Step 6: Review Technical Infrastructure: Explore New Technology as an Aid to Responsive Service Delivery

The provision of law services has come along way from the quill pen and
parchment. Yet many organizations experience difficulties because of a
lack of basic information technology infrastructure. One interview with a
partner of a leading London law firm recounted the regular problem his
firm had in losing law reports and handbooks. Much time and money were
wasted in repeatedly searching for reports that were missing or in someone's briefcase or office. Regular moratoriums were declared in order to
replenish the depleted central library resources.

Technology can be deployed to overcome these difficulties and provide on-line libraries where law reports can be accessed over local-area
networks or as part of a subscription service. Systems do exist, but they are
somewhat unfriendly and have overlooked the emotional and historical
attachment that lawyers have to the physical law report. A system where
an image of the report in question could be viewed (as in a library) and the
pages turned "on-line" by the lawyer would be a significant step forward.
Such a culturally sensitive implementation would encourage the use of
new technology within this traditional profession.

Another area of review is the medium through which a legal department or office receives instructions and delivers advice. There is no logical reason why the legal department needs to maintain face-to-face encounters with its customers. Email and group conferencing can allow law advice to be provided anywhere, anytime, at least in preparatory stages. Consistent with the agile principle of leveraging resources, wholehearted use of enterprise communications would allow specialized law expertise to be available whenever and wherever it is needed in the enterprise.

The first step to more widespread acceptance of IT and communication tools for lawyers is training. Too often, unfamiliarity with technology and how it can be used creates yet another barrier between the business and its legal department.

Step 7: Develop a Program of Regular New Practice Scenarios

What is advocated here cannot be a one-off activity, but must become an ongoing process by which the legal department or independent law office continually seeks ways to be agile and proactive in its delivery of timely services. As such, a creative process must be settled upon through which ongoing problems can be tackled and solutions designed by those involved.

One possible approach is to convene a group of lawyers and customers who share a common interest in new agile law services and how these can propel the business forward. Such a group can regularly convene to define and explore new problems and new agile law services to solve these problems. Its output is an outline action plan that describes the business benefits from the changes proposed. This can be used to frame the ongoing journey for the law function and its interaction with its customers.

The convening of such a group and the conduct of new practice scenarios can, of course, be virtual as well as face to face. Group conferencing is a very appropriate media through which to conduct these deliberations, one that does not incur cost and travel penalties and in which a record of the discussion is maintained.

Step 8: Implement a Comprehensive Intellectual Property Asset Inventory

One practical and valuable contribution that a law function can undertake for an enterprise that is going agile is the creation of an intellectual property asset inventory.[3] Working in conjunction with the business unit, it is possible to identify the explicit intellectual property (patents, trademarks, licenses, etc.) as well as the tacit intellectual property (know-how, ideas, copyright, etc.).

Understanding whether a particular asset

- produces an economic advantage
- raises a barrier to competition, or
- creates or defends a strong market position

or any combination of the three, helps the business to determine the value of the asset and to develop a plan to exploit it appropriately. A joint goal may be to achieve a year-on-year asset inventory increase of 25% through collaborative activities with customers or suppliers. It may also include a disposal strategy whereby intellectual assets are systematically disposed of for profit if the economic value to the firm falls below a predetermined threshold.

Step 9: Change the Reward Structure to Reinforce New Behavior

As with any agile change, reward and compensation procedures need to be aligned with the new behavior that is required. If management, engineering, marketing, and training professionals, to name but a few, are rewarded on the basis of their value added to the agile enterprise, rather than their adherence to job descriptions, it becomes difficult to argue that lawyers should be treated differently.

Evaluation

It may be useful to undertake an evaluation of the performance change in transitioning to an agile law service. This will require defining measures of the existing state and then to revisiting these over time to assess progress. Suggested measures could include the following:

- Responsiveness to the business (possibly measured by customer satisfaction reports)
- Drafting ratios
- Reusability of precedents and standard agreements
- Increase in intellectual asset base, and the like

---

3. We talked about an inventory of intellectual property in Chapter 9 in the context of knowledge management, in Chapter 8 in the context of information confidentiality on intranets, and in Chapter 4 in the context of proficiency in partnering.

Summary

We have indicated here a number of changes in the business environment that will create change for corporations' legal departments and for individual law practices. Key among these are the changes created by networking, particularly the Internet. Our message is that the commercial law profession is not protected from the changes that are facing the rest of industry. Neither is there any compelling reason why they should be protected nor for their customers to regard them as protected. The transitions needed for these law operations to add value and survive are in principle those of agility.

The opportunity exists through a series of cultural, business and technological changes, which we have outlined in a set of nine steps, to transform the nature of in-house and independent law services' provision in ways that will add significant business value. In so doing, criticism and cynicism of the past toward the law function can be dispelled. An agile law service will become a full partner in the agile business.

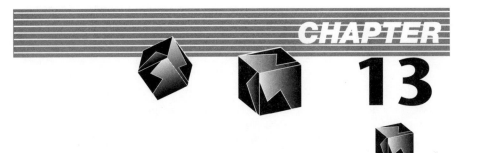

AGILE MANAGEMENT

We need agile management, not remote control.
—Glen Tines, Hewlett-Packard

In this short chapter, we shall take a highly focused view of the purpose and tasks of the agile manager. We concentrate on how managers support agile teams, since teams are the building blocks of agility. We shall be controversial in order to counteract prevailing orthodoxies.

Given the complexity of the modern organization, much management time is consumed in things like budgets and reporting. At times it seems to us that agility and management are oxymorons, at least the way management often operates today. We know it's human nature that what were once "means" turn, over time, into "ends." For example, there is a current fixation on searching out core competencies. This is largely about rooting through support activities that have taken on a life of their own in order to discover what actually creates competitive value. Management is one of those means that has become its own end. How many more books are written about management than about how to work? From our perspective, agile management isn't as much about budgets and reports as it is about helping work teams sustain the agility that they need to get work done in the face of change.

189

Management Is Helping to Get the Work Done

Management often forgets that its raison d'être is primarily to help the work get done. In practice, not just in theory. The halls of industry are filled with managers who have eagerly signed up for empowering their people. This usually means abandoning them to their own devices and spending their time managing upward—this is thought to pay better returns in terms of careers advancement. Likewise in academia. Research, publishing, and sitting on committees ought to be means to the end of enhancing the transfer of knowledge to learners (that is, teaching). Instead, they feed the pragmatic end of career survival.

This misdirected model of management can be seen graphically as the organizational pyramid, with the hierarchies of management at the top. Figure 13–1 offers an alternative view, the inverted pyramid. This puts the real function of management, indeed the whole value chain of the agile organization, in better perspective. According to this view, management becomes a service to work teams, and not the other way round.

The role for management in agility is to make it possible for teams to do all the agile networking things that we're discussing in this book. The model agile manager is more of a coach than a bureaucrat. He or she has the responsibility—and accountability—for preparing teams to agilely engage in their work and supporting them in the face of change.

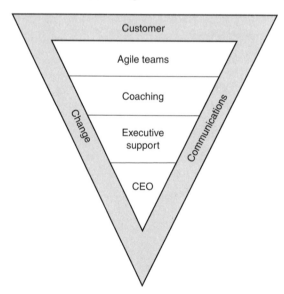

Figure 13–1 The Agile Management Pyramid.

Prepare is the key word. A well-prepared team executes its work much better than an ad hoc group that tries to play together under the real-time instruction of a screaming sideline coach.

Visualize a scenario. You're a striker in an important soccer game. You and your teammates are talented (competent), have practiced (trained), played together (had teaming experience), and pretty much know how to adapt to circumstances in mounting an attack. You take into consideration the weather, the pitch, the score, the stage of the game, the efforts of the defense, and so on, and move the ball within the scope of the boundaries and the rules. So you are agile, and midway through the game you score.

Now consider this. In irregular sequence, the following happens. It starts to hail. The field doubles in size. Another team joins the game against you and your opponent. Half of your teammates are replaced by people you don't know. Ninety percent of the remaining time is taken off the clock. Do you score?

An absurd example? Perhaps, but many of us have felt just this midway into a project. Does it help to have the coach shout directions from the sidelines? On the other hand, did your preparation to deal with change help? Well, maybe not a lot, but you see the point.

Six Tasks for Agile Managers

There is a lot management can and must do to support agile teams. And we've seen indicators of these responsibilities in earlier chapters. Management needs to:

1. Set the vision and strategy for the team
2. Understand organizational competencies
3. Drive the design of the operations or work system
4. Provide the infrastructure to support the teams
5. Keep the agile work system in balance
6. Evaluate and revisit the strategies and competencies

But this is all pretty standard. What's different? What's agile about this management charge?

Well, first, we mean it. Nowhere in the list do we see the following implied:

- "Harass the troops with constant requests for updates."
- "Make sure that everyone shows up, in person or electronically, for the weekly 'information sharing' staff meetings."
- "Never be available."
- "Be so occupied with weekly budgeting fire drills that the only time you communicate with working teams is during the annual team-building exercise when you tell everyone that 'people are our most important asset.' "

And we can't emphasize this enough. In recent months the slick business press has made a lot out of virtual or remote management. We are led to believe that visionary managers have broken the code of helping virtual teams do great things—even though these teams are out of the line of sight. But, invariably, what's offered up is an anecdotal account of how someone manages to sustain a managerial presence while squirreled away on some remote mountaintop, looking at the sunset and firing off emails from his or her laptop to hapless recipients around the world. As Glen Tines of Hewlett-Packard puts it, "What these people are really talking about is 'remote control,' not 'remote management.' " Click. And the point of the story is usually to sell modems or laptops, not to contribute to the lore of effective management in a virtual environment.[1]

OK, enough, what should agile managers be doing? The six basic management responsibilities listed previously provide as good a framework as any for approaching agile management. But we'll do something different here by looking at each of these in reverse order. That way we'll move from visible effects to what it takes conceptually to get these effects. Besides, organizations are already at work, with strategies, missions, and competencies in place. It's more agile to work from the concrete of what exists than the theoretical of what might be.

---

1. The next time someone tries to sell you "virtual management technology" you should ask them three questions. First, will they do a value-priced solution-based deal, where they take a cut of your increased profits (or lowered costs)? Second, ask them to throw in training in best practices for virtual management using this technology. Third, ask for figures that show the proportion of their managers working this way, and then ask to talk to some of them.

Figure 13–2 illustrates the overall approach. There are two important points.

1. We refer to "you" in the following. In fact this "you" is the manager facilitating this methodology with his or her work team. The methodology progress with the involvement of the work team, not by the manager alone.

2. As with any methodology that deals with complexity and people, sequence is pretty much an illusion. At all stages of the process you will need to interact with all other stages. Not neat or easy, but realistic.

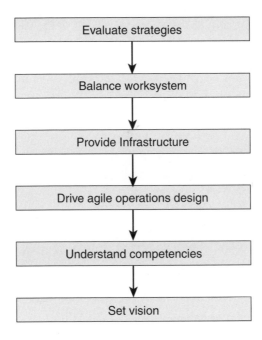

Figure 13–2 Agile Networking Management Cycle.

1. Evaluate and Revisit the Strategies and Competencies

Most organizations are in midstream or better on some projects or programs. A good way to begin managing agile work teams is to take a look at these finishing conditions and evaluate how things went in terms of the agile networking. Recall that in Chapter 6 we suggested a scorecard for evaluating agile networking. This was a matrix that mapped standard agility change domains against agile networking capabilities. Figure 13–3 presents an example of that matrix used as a scorecard. The agile networking scorecard can be used in this way.

First, review and evaluate one or more teaming initiatives in terms of (1) what worked well and what didn't work and (2) opportunities and barriers to getting work done agilely. Analyze these aspects of the project or program and map them to the appropriate cell in the matrix. Start with just a few, maybe a half-dozen. For example, you might come up with the following:

a. We repeatedly had to send people off for training in mid-project, costing us time and money.

b. Management reviews ate up too much time.

c. It took too long to find technical information when we needed it.

d. We couldn't change our work processes when things altered.

e. Our conferencing system helped to save us travel time and money.

f. We managed document revisions much better than before.

g. The web-page based beta-test and marketing approach worked well.

Then give each a value from 1 (terrible) to 9 (excellent). Try not to use 4, 5, or 6—dwell in the extremes. Map these values into the scorecard and look for where excellence exists or effort is needed. Then go back and map a few more entries; this time it's okay to use 4, 5, and 6. When the matrix looks pretty well populated, you can begin working on balancing your agile networking capabilities.

Networking Capability

Agility Change Domain	Group Communication	Intranet Publishing	Knowledge Management	Learning Services	Teaming	Management
Creation			3			7
Capacity						
Capability						
Reconfiguration	2				8	
Migration						
Performance	8	8				2
Improvement						
Recovery						

Figure 13–3 Agile networking scorecard.

195

2. Keep the Agile Work System in Balance

Next look for patterns, the aspects of good or not-so-good agile performance that seem to cluster. Especially find areas where agile networking capabilities in one area are transferable to another. In what columns are there both high- and low-value cells? For example, why not use web-based learning services delivered to the desktop, instead of sending people off to courses? Can the web expertise that supported field test and marketing be turned to "web sleuthing," using the web to find information and track down the experts in leading-edge research? Be creative—find a few high-leverage areas and decide to invest there on your next effort.

Here is where you can look at your resources: the competencies you have available either internally or through alliances. Indeed, good agile management can counter poor response from an internal function by raising the possibility of going outside. For most knowledge-based competencies, networking has made it just as easy to work with people outside as with people inside. It has created an environment in which internal competencies compete with external competencies on a level playing field.[2] There's no need to succumb to the tyranny of internal, single-source recalcitrance or greed when the outside option is available. If training, or legal, or IT don't want to support the team effort, hire outside competencies. Sometimes just the possibility of having to compete with outside providers helps internal groups to recognize agile realities and improve their performance.[3]

3. Provide the Infrastructure to Support the Teams

The agile improvements you choose to invest in may require added infrastructure: not just technology, but training and perhaps greater awareness of the need for an agility culture.

Raise the visibility of agile successes and make the direction of investment clear. Perhaps it's time to go for wider-bandwidth LANs, to roll out robust group conferencing and intranet publication systems, to hire a

2. In Chapter 14, we further demolish the boundary between inside and outside the organization.

3. In Chapter 11, we talked about a transition for the training department to a provider of agile learning services. In Chapter 12, a transition for the legal department to a provider of agile legal services was discussed. The pattern should be coming clear. An agile enterprise needs all its functions to operate agilely. Internal functions need to see the rest of the enterprise as the customer for its services, whose value is rated by the customer not the provider.

webmaster, to provide laptops for everyone that travels. We all know technology is good, but acquisition should be based on solid investment needs. And, remember, it's very easy today to lease technology and telecommunications (including web connectivity services) if, for whatever reason, support is not forthcoming from the internal IT/telecoms group.[4]

4. Drive the Design of the Operations or Work System

This stage involves looking at the potential of the agile networking capabilities and infrastructure and designing a work system that will create optimum value in the face of change. Let's repeat that. Here is where the agile manager explicitly builds in the capabilities to reconfigure the work processes in the face of change. Consider what internal or external events could occur. What impact would these have on the work? How can processes respond to this change?

In looking at the team's potential for change, the congruence of networking and agility will show its practical value. As discussed in Chapter 6, networking allows nodes and links to switch as purposes change, or links as nodes change. Thus the agile team's responsiveness to change is enhanced by being networked.

The motto "those who do the work, design the work" holds here, but it's management's responsibility to see that work design happens. Given time pressures, it's tempting but wrong to go right into the work without designing the processes: the communications, work processes, change processes, and learning systems that will support the teams through the initiative.

How to do this? One of the best approaches to agile design is through modeling. A visual modeling tool captures the people, process, product and technology aspects of an initiative. It allows management to establish a clear picture of what's going on and how it can be reconfigured. As we said in Chapter 3, knowledge about how processes fit together is as important in the agile world as knowledge about the processes themselves.

While a spreadsheet or simple database with a graphics front end will do, more sophisticated systems are emerging that enable management to

---

4. Consistent with the idea that internal functions should migrate to agile service providers, the IT department is an excellent candidate for such transition. This doesn't just mean it's outsourced and customer focused. It means it understands agile competition.

create networked models that are hot-linked right into the real-time work environment. For example, a project model may show the communications infrastructure that supports, say, approval of the marketing plan. At any time during the project, management can look at that model, click on an artifact such as "team release conference," and immediately pop into the actual group conference that is the workplace for release dialogue. This capability has enormous benefits, including the following:

- Management always has real-time news of project status.
- Teams are spared the need to constantly explain and report "how things are going."
- Audit trails of performance are automatically provided.

5. Understand Organizational Competencies

By now you should have a good idea of what the required organizational and people competencies are and which ones need to be developed or acquired. Competencies aren't things we say we can do; they are what we have demonstrated. When you understand what you can do now or will be able to do shortly, you can look to the vision and strategies and see if they are achievable.

6. Set the Vision and Strategy for the Team

At this point you have a only couple of choices: either accept your vision and strategies and build or buy the competencies needed to execute then (for example, create alliances), or be pragmatic and modify your vision and strategies. One way or another, these need to align if you want to succeed. A "stretch" vision is commendable, but it must be approachable to have any value.

Management and Coaching as an Agile Core Competency

If the expectations on management are that anyone can do it, then there will be serious problems in trying to create and sustain organizational agility. Indeed, if management is seen as an undifferentiated commodity service, it will not be long before it's subject to agile competition. We see this already. Many enterprises hire external management consultants. Often these people aren't consulting so much as managing. They represent a management service that is bought from outside. Hence internal managers already face competition from outside suppliers. For management to differentiate itself in an agile environment, managers need to equip themselves with the skills of agile management, as outlined here. Then management becomes a core competency, to be developed and even placed under the remit of knowledge management.

Agile managers need to understand the benefits and challenges of agility. To succeed, their knowledge, skills, commitment, and experience must go far beyond the commodity preparation that they receive even in good MBA programs. Managers may not be at the top of the agile organizational pyramid, but it will surely collapse if they do not pull their weight.

Summary

This chapter has taken a highly focused view of the role of the manager in the agile enterprise. We propose that the correct way to view management is as a service to work teams and that the purpose of management and the role of managers is to help the work to get done. A six-step methodology, based on a scorecard approach, allows agile managers to strategize their support to work teams. Agile mangers should look both outside and inside the enterprise for the support services that they need, especially if internal functions aren't agile. However, management itself could become regarded as a commodity service, purchasable from anywhere. The alternative is to develop agile management as a differentiated, core competency of the agile enterprise.

4

Agile
Networked
Enterprise

We've spent some time discussing the environment that has given rise to agile networking, as well as the capabilities that enterprises should develop in order to provide agile solutions to their customers. Now we'll look at where these capabilities are put to use in the agile operations of organizations.

First, in Chapter 14, we'll discuss agile alliances, how and why they work and how they underpin agile networking. Then, in succeeding chapters, we'll look at commerce and education, two major areas in which agile networking can and must contribute value. In each case, we'll be structuring our argument around basic agility principles: the need to compete in rapid change, meeting niche market demand for solutions, leveraging competencies and technologies, and collaboration. And we'll be approaching the networking dimension according to the basic principles we established earlier in the book: nodes, links, and switching.

continued on next page

Underlying much of the discussion in this part are the complementary phenomena of disaggregation and aggregation. Information technology and networks have enabled us to deal with
ever more minute pieces of data. Where once high-level or batch
feedback was provided, today detailed data are readily available.
A restaurant chain can track the temperatures of its ovens across
the globe; retail inventories are updated with every point of sale
purchase; instead of income brackets, individuals and demographic subgroups constitute niche markets. Conversely, aggregation helps to pool competencies into value building initiatives:
individuals work in teams; companies work in virtual organizations, or alliances.

In a way, agile networking enterprise involves striking a balance
between the great and the small, the aggregated organizational
capabilities and customer solutions made possible by identifying
discrete competencies and niche markets. Networking enables
the enterprise to be agile within and across the domains of supply and demand.

AGILE NETWORKED ALLIANCES

Agility makes special mention of virtual organizations. The agile principle of cooperating to compete, described in Chapter 4, is all about gaining proficiency in building and operating in virtual organizations. For simplicity's sake, we used the generic term partnerships there to describe these organizational forms.

In this chapter, we shall look at virtual organization forms and other products of the practice of cooperating to compete, under the title of agile alliances. We use the term alliance to describe a wide variety of cooperative working arrangements.

Let's take time to remind ourselves of why alliances are so important to agility. Today's business environment is dominated by change, complexity, and demands for rapid concept to cash cycles. Enriching the customer with a variety of business-to-business solutions and niche products is becoming an entry requirement to doing business. Mastering change is a requirement, not an option, for survival. Leveraging resources mobilizes what the enterprise owns to bottom-line benefit, but also reveals the gap between the resources it needs and those that it owns. How else but through alliances can an organization quickly secure all the competencies needed to compress a product cycle to precisely meet a greater variety of customer needs? In an age where speed and rapid adaptation is the hall-mark of winning, can companies, who believe that they own all the answers and resources, prosper? Before we begin discussing specific agile alliances, three notes.

First, there is a common misperception that any enterprise that is a partner in an alliance is therefore agile. That alliances equal agility. This misperception has been nailed by recent investigations by the Agile Oper-ations Group of The Agility Forum. These investigations have revealed that external relations—outsourcing or partnering—are not the defining vari-able of agility. According to Sue Hartman, who managed the year-long action research project,

> Evidence shows that what really determines agility is how well agile com-petencies and agile best practices align with an agile strategy. Whether or not the organization implements an outsourcing or a vertical integration strategy is less important.

Thus it's your capability that makes you agile, not whether you have an external alliance.

Second, it's helpful to consider not only external relationships, but also internal relationships, as alliances. This is because, in reality, the boundary between external and internal is often not significant. (We expand on this later as one of the assumptions about alliances that needs to be challenged.) In reality, the difference between internal and external alliances is less important than how alliances are formed and what they do. Thus here we define agile alliances to include the strategies and opera-tions that support *internal* (cross-functional) as well as *external* alliances.

Third, and following on from considering alliances to be both inter-nal and external, it will be remembered that in Chapter 10 we discussed the emergence of virtual and agile teams. Much of that discussion is appli-cable in describing agile alliances. Agile alliances, too, have been prod-ucts of increasing rates of change and complexity, although at strategic rather than tactical levels. And, like agile teams, today's agile alliances operate under a different set of assumptions than have traditional alliances.

Let's start with comparing the old and new assumptions about alli-ances. From there we shall look at different types of alliance, the network-ing capabilities that today's alliance partners need.

Alliances: The Old Assumptions

Historically, alliances have been a vital tool for management. They have provided a workable strategy through which an enterprise can share the resources and risk needed to address market needs. The method and practice of alliance management is well understood and documented. It describes a broad family of commercial and legal frameworks through which the goals and objectives of the corporate manager can be achieved. However, traditional alliances have thrived in a much more stable environment than we have today. Things changed more slowly, and organizations could take time to create the process, the cultural and technological arrangements that would foster collaboration. Unfortunately, building alliances in slow time is not a luxury available to today's management. Nevertheless, success stories abound, be they in building market share, or developing new lines of business, or meeting the needs of complex niche markets. Alliances are here to stay, but they will be different in an agile world.

As a basis for considering agile alliances, we will look at four powerful assumptions that shape and underpin our thinking on alliances. These are the beliefs that we need to "unlearn" before we can fully realize the agility potential of alliances.

Assumption 1: Strategic Alliances Take a Long Time to Create. Therefore, Limit the Number That You Engage in

Most of us can form a mental picture of a continuum of alliances. It ranges from simple contractual relationships to complicated collaboration, joint venture, and minority shareholding arrangements. Generally, we assume that the more important an alliance is, the longer it will take to formulate.

It is unlikely (and unheard of) for a joint venture to be concluded within a matter a weeks. The "concept to cash" time of such ventures is measured in months or years. We have become conditioned to thinking that this will always be the case. Indeed, it seems that if lawyers don't ensure that this is so then the organizational bureaucracy can be counted on to keep the wheels of alliance grinding exceedingly slowly.

The delays, committees, process hurdles, and other barriers that exist within organizations have been established by well-meaning, well-intentioned folk. Their main concern is lowering risk: avoiding mistakes and overcommitments from which the organization will not be able to escape.

Or at least extricate itself only with great pain and cost. Thus we have the mental barrier that it's impossible to move rapidly into a joint venture or strategic alliance.

Assumption 2: Complex Alliances Are Difficult to Dissolve

"Marry in haste; repent at leisure" is the enduring adage. Fearful of entering into complicated arrangements because of the inability to dissolve them swiftly if things go wrong, managers avoid entanglements entirely. It is true that legal formalities require great diligence and effort to disassemble. An organizational marriage is much easier to achieve than an organizational divorce. There's no Reno where disenchanted partners can unload their opposite numbers in a fast-track, no-fault dissolution. The difficulty of the end game causes many to shy away from any engagement at all.

Assumption 3: Alliances Are Founded on Win–Win Premises

Conventional wisdom states that one of the major reasons alliances founder is because of the failure of one party to ensure that the other is successful. The imbalance in payoff leads to distrust and dissatisfaction, and soon the deal is off. We assume, therefore, that win–win must be a core value of all alliances. This complicates alliance negotiations. Most parties really don't know the value propositions of the other partners and can only guess at what their "win" would be.

Assumption 4: Alliances Are External

We naturally think of dealing with an external entity when we consider an alliance. We have a mental picture of a boundary that separates internal from external. However, if we consider just three components of this boundary, we see that the distinction between external and internal blurs.

1. We picture the boundary as some level of difficulty in forming an alliance. However, it's often much easier to form an alliance with an external partner than an internal partner. Turf wars, for example, are far less frequent in external partnerships than internal.

2. If the boundary is seen as based on the distinction between our budget and their budget, business unit cost centers make the same distinction internally. Our budget is just as separate from someone else's, be they internal or external.

3. The boundary between external and internal may be believed to represent some level of difficulty of communication. However, we point to the ubiquity of networks—Internet and extranets (networks of intranets)—in allowing rich cross-enterprise communication.

So alliances are alliances, regardless of whether they are internal or external.

Agile Alliances: The New Assumptions

Enterprises must shift their thinking, approach, and practices regarding partnering and alliances to create value that constantly, innovatively enriches their customers. Much of what we know today about alliances and alliance management must be jettisoned and dismantled. In a world of agile competition, it needs to be replaced by a new system of cooperation that is based on radical rethinking of partnering. This new system is supported by the advances in process knowledge and technology that help to overcome the barriers implicit in our assumptions.

We'll posit first as hypotheses some new assumptions, or mental models, about alliances. Then we'll explore some of the characteristics of agile alliances, enabled through agile networking. Finally, we'll look at some different types of alliances that have emerged through agile networking.

Assumption 1: Do Alliances Quickly; Do Them Often

True agile partnering will see an explosion in all aspects of alliances. The number of alliances, the number of partners, and the value of alliances will increase. Moreover, their duration will be compressed. Operating agilely will require an organization to retain the flexibility to change and respond to new customer needs and external forces in a way that cannot be constrained by rigid relationships. While long-term relationships will persist as important strategic backdrops, by far the greatest number of alliances will be centered on short-lived customer-enriching programs. If the old world was characterized by "marriage," the new could be seen as a move toward "brief affairs."

Assumption 2: Alliances Should Be Concluded the Moment That They Deliver Their Value

As with virtual teams, the ability to dissolve is the corollary of the ability to form. Swift dissolution of alliances and relationships will be essential to success. Paradoxically, an organization's ability to conclude a partnership with alacrity will increase the likelihood of further alliances with these same partners. A reputation for being able quickly to dissolve one alliance and get on with the next will be valued.

Assumption 3: Each Organization Must Focus on "Win"

The notion of win–win relationships is deceptive. In truth most organizations focus on "win" rather than "win–win." This is not to say that they expect the other partners to lose. Rather, they leave it to them to figure out their own wins. Every partner will be expected to take responsibility for achieving its goals. Perhaps, as the trading world places more emphasis on responsibility and less on mutuality, we'll be learning to "compete to cooperate."

Assumption 4: Alliances Are Internal and External

The distinction between internal and external is increasingly blurring. It's often easier to form an alliance with an external partner than an internal partner. At least between enterprises there is a clean sheet and legal structures to provide framework. Internally, old grudges, turf wars, wrong assumptions, and budget competition often torpedo alliances.

Indeed, managers in organizations that find that it is easier to make deals outside than inside may like to consider why. Could it be a lack of agility? In Chapter 4, we described the agile principle of cooperating to compete. We talked of building proficiency in partnering and facility in operating a virtual organization. We can now see that these strategies apply not only to external alliances, but also to internal alliances. An organizational unit that wishes to be agile should consider adopting these strategies in both its internal and external dealing.

Types of Agile Alliances

Now we'll look briefly at some of the more popular types of alliances in which agile enterprises engage to meet near-term, but strategic goals. The first three, cross-functional work, outsourcing, and partnering, have been around a lot longer than agility. They are mentioned here only from the perspective of how they can play in achieving agility. The fourth, aggregation, is a recent agile phenomenon that is both logically and technically supported by networking. Last, but perhaps most powerful for the future, is the agile web, a unique and rapidly developing artifact of agility.

Cross-functional Work

We've mentioned that agility need not involve external alliances. It can involve interdepartmental alliances that lead to cross-functional working. In such alliances, staff from, for example, marketing, engineering, production, logistics, and sales come together in one team to create the product life cycle. Operations are collaborative and concurrent across these previously stovepiped functions. And in creating these cross-functional operations, new alliances have to be created between internal functions.

Cross-functional work has been around a long time; for example, concurrent engineering has been successful over the past two decades. Today the emergence of corporate networking has greatly enhanced the potential for collaborative internal work. It overcomes the barrier caused by separate functions being in different places. If marketing is in St. Louis and manufacturing in Atlanta, how do you create a cross-functional team without massive travel or relocation expense? The answer lies in the network.

Outsourcing

During the past few years, outsourcing has become a popular factor in the downsizing equation. As the concept of identifying core and noncore competencies caught on, many enterprises figured out that they could do better by unloading service groups that provided nondifferentiating competencies or services and leasing the service for that competency from external organizations that could do it better, cheaper, and faster.

Why have a direct sales catalogue division if you can hire L. L. Bean? Why have a training group if you can hire a university proficient in just-in-time learning? Why do preliminary research if you can hire a private lab? With the total interoperability of voice, data, and information networks, the outsourced entity, while being physically and organizationally separate, can operate seamlessly in the same workspace as the enterprise.

But a second issue has arisen with outsourcing. Of late it's become unfashionable to treat product or component suppliers like, well, suppliers. This is a result of the old assumption thinking about win–win relationships. However, organizations that have developed agile practices to effect and manage outsourcing have no trouble operating in this mode. They know that both vendor and supplier will understand the metrics for their own success and can form fast contractual arrangements.

Partnering

"Partner" is another hot word. More lofty than "supplier," it suggests strategic involvement. And true partnerships do just that. Here risk is shared in the form of up-front investment, equity sharing, and high-level links across organizations. We've seen short-term partnerships in the advertising world that have operated through daily CEO videoconferences. Group conferencing supports strategic partnerships in the high-tech and communications industries.

And partnering, especially in high tech, has taken some bizarre turns. Noting Microsoft's® very agile investment in arch rival Apple™, one observer noted: "In a paradox peculiar to the industry, the fast pace of technology has forced rivals into a dizzying array of alliances to get access to the latest software and computer advances from the other side—technology they neither have the cash, time or resources to develop alone."[1]

Aggregation

Aggregation is a phenomenon made possible by two phenomena: ubiquitous networking connectivity and access to discrete information. Aggregators are organizations that create integrated solution services for customers out of what were formally disparate components. For example, because of economic conditions, a securities firm expects a short-lived, but intense flow of stock market share investments into real estate. The firm creates organizational relationships and extranet links to providers of the discrete elements of realty: on-line real estate listings, geodemographic and educational information, real-time mortgage and insurance rates, and regional cultural data. The aggregator sets up an "Investland" web site and lists it in the appropriate web search engines, as well as in print media sent out with investor statements. An agile team drawn from the participating component organizations designs and manages the service entirely on-line. When the time niche expires, so does the aggregated entity.

Aggregation provides an interesting counterpoint to the continuing interest in "molecularization" of products, services, and competencies. As smaller and smaller units of value or capability are recognized, the possibilities for recombination are increased. Witness the strides forward in

1. David K. Kalish, "Apple's Enemies Have Reason to Save It, " *New Hampshire Sunday News*, August 10, 1997, p. D–1.

DNA recombinant engineering. Aggregators identify elements of value at low levels and combine them in new forms under a single interface to satisfy new markets.

Webs

The web metaphor has relevance to agility far beyond the reaches of the Internet World Wide Web. Networking, in the sense of agile teaming relationships, certainly captures the essence of the web: peer-to-peer connectivity, with ready access to alternative nodes through alternative paths. A web is a structure of competencies, which can be accessed and aggregated to collaboratively create value.

Indeed, the term "Agile Web" has been taken as its trademark by a group of small manufacturing companies in eastern Pennsylvania. With the guidance and support of the Ben Franklin Institute of Technology in Lehigh, the Agile Web, Inc., enables "the rapid formation of a dynamic combination of companies, selected for each opportunity." BFIT helped the individual companies in this select group to define agile strategies and provided them with common training on agility. The companies work together under a set of contractual and ethical guidelines to identify market opportunities, pull together the needed competencies within the pool, and deliver customer solutions. They make extensive use of electronic data interchange and email in transacting business. At this writing they have been very successful in pulling together fast-track solutions to customer needs from member competencies.

The Networking Institute of Newton, Massachusetts, is at the eye of another kind of agile web. They maintain a web site called Netage that contains links to their robust set of virtual teaming and networking services: writing, speaking, and consulting. But, more than this, there are graphical links to the home pages of organizations that provide complementary competencies: networking software, training, teaming, and organizational development. A potential customer can initiate on the spot all the relationships needed for a solution in specific networked teaming situations, reducing time to customer satisfaction dramatically.

Enabled by the spread of connectivity and the understanding of interorganizational relationships, webs of all kinds will become a dominant organizational form in the 21st century.

Agile Networking Capabilities for Alliances

It is very difficult to conceive of alliances in the late 1990s that do not involve some degree of networking. Of the types of alliance that we have reviewed, webs and aggregators are based on and require networking infrastructure. Partnerships and outsourcing alliances do not logically require networking, but are unlikely to succeed as alliances or as businesses without it. The level of connectivity required between alliance partners in today's business environment demands a networking component. We have come a long way from "consortium teams," who would gather daily in a shared office to pursue their work.

- The geographic spread of alliances now means that they cannot do their work unless networked. Because alliances are formed to get access to resources that are not currently owned, it's a defeating condition that the only resources that can be got at are local. Today's alliances form among partners that have complementary competencies, regardless of geography.
- Of course, people can travel, can't they? Well, maybe, but for how long, how far, and at how much budgetary and psychological cost? Do we limit the skills we can use in an alliance to those owned by young unattached people who "wouldn't mind a few weeks away from home at the company's expense"?
- And today's professionals are multitasked. It's rare to find people with the needed competencies who do not have other responsibilities that tie them to their home base or other locations. Are alliance teams to be made up of people who have nothing else to do?

Networking allows today's alliances to work. Certainly, they may involve travel and temporary relocation by a few staff. But far more of the work of the alliance happens in and on the network, connecting people wherever they are.

Thus networking capabilities are vital to alliance partners. We describe here the networking capabilities that are essential to making agile alliances work.

1. Agile networking behavior
2. Inventorying intellectual assets

3. Understanding organizational "footprints"

4. Streamlining approval and review processes

We will consider each of these capabilities in turn.

1. Agile Networking Behavior

It almost goes without saying that agile networking is essential for agile alliances to prosper. Expectations should be set early on that the values of agility will be clearly visible in the goals of the alliance and that the network will be a major instrument of value creation.

The way to go about this is to select key processes and design and implement them as agile networked processes, like those described in earlier chapters. Ask what it is about an alliance that means that its work should not have the network support that internal work would have? If the response is that we don't have the technology to do this, then consider going outside for a technology service. At the time of writing, a number of independent web services providers exist who can host group conference, web pages, and even web-based learning tools. These services share a common interface across platforms and are only a URL and password away from everyone in the alliance. We can predict that these *connectivity providers* will multiply and supply increasingly sophisticated services to alliances.

Such an alliance intranet, hosted in-house or externally, readily becomes the alliance's shared workspace. For example:

- Create channels for open communication among peer workers in each alliance partner. It's a no-brainer to supply email connectivity, but what about shared group conferences accessible by all alliance partners?
- Create web conferences that support cross-functional teams composed of partner members.
- Make in-house "confidential" intranet pages accessible to partners. The reason? So that partners get a better understanding of the structure of each others' businesses and how they can provide joint solutions.
- Use an alliance intranet to publish alliance documents, protocols, standards, and deliverables.

• Create collaborative knowledge-management systems in defined areas.
• Make joint learning opportunities available to all partners through cross-partner agile learning services.

As organizations begin to appreciate the values of agility, extending the range of agile networking operations will become less of a struggle.

2. Inventorying Intellectual Assets

As we said in Chapter 4, developing a clear view of the value of the items of the enterprise's intellectual property will speed not only the enterprise's ability to form alliances, but also their attractiveness as an alliance partner.

However, surprisingly few enterprises possess any clear view of the true value of their intellectual property. If any, they have focused on the intellectual property assets more widely understood and registered as trademarks and patents. They have ignored the vast ocean of a valuable intellectual property asset—knowledge.

We described earlier, in Chapter 9, outline steps for the agile enterprise to inventory its knowledge. These comprised asking questions that reveal the value of knowledge, for example, "What would the impact be to your customers if you did not have this knowledge?" and "What would the impact be to you if this knowledge were in a competitor's enterprise and not in yours?" Then ask what is the time horizon of that knowledge, recognizing that the half-life of useful knowledge in the agile enterprise is short.

There is also a new spin in the networked world: the impact of networking on the valuing and protection of intellectual property. We don't have answers here, but can convey the perspective.

Many people hold the position that trading within the digital economy has challenged our long-standing views on sharing material, information, and intellectual assets. The seminal work on this subject was written by John Perry Barlow, lyricist for the Grateful Dead and co-founder of the Electronic Frontier Foundation.[2] He argues powerfully that much of what we know about intellectual property is wrong and that success in the networked, digital world will come through greater sharing and collaboration of ideas.

---

2. John Perry Barlow, "Selling Wine without Bottles: The Economy of Mind in the Global Net" (1993). Available from the web site of The Electronic Frontier Foundation.

He also maintains that a new cultural, ethical, and technological (rather than legal) system will arise and govern behavior regarding intellectual property. That is, the Internet will be a force for general change in the way that we regard intellectual property.

It is also worth remembering that partners enter into agile alliances to gain access to resources that they do not currently have. If the resources sought are one partners' intellectual property, then overprotection rather than a collaborative stance may simply kill off the alliance. Your intellectual property assets, in the context of an alliance, may be just what your partners are looking for. Hence inventorying and valuing them is sound commercial practice.

So, by developing an asset inventory the enterprise makes a major step toward being able to effectively develop agile alliances. The ability to seize opportunities and proactively seek new partners to enrich its clients will be a winning capability prized within the agile economy.

3. Understanding Organizational "Footprints"

All organizations possess a shape or a footprint. This footprint is the system of vision, culture, processes, values, technologies, and knowledge. However, this footprint is rarely sensed, especially from inside the organization. The inability to recognize the "home" footprint leads to difficulty in identifying fit with partners.

Developing a mental model and picture of the organization's own footprint and why it is attractive to partners will become increasingly valued. Equally, the ability to assess potential partners' footprints will be increasingly important.

One key attribute that an enterprise needs to understand about its own footprint and look for in others' footprints is its agile networking capabilities. When, as we have said, alliance almost equals networked, enterprises without networking capability will be viewed as poor potential partners. Note that this does not mean that the enterprise has to own substantial networking systems. The technology is available from third-party web service providers. Rather than technology, the issue is networking behavior and mental models. Regardless of the technology it owns, an enterprise without a culture of networking will be a poor partner in network-based alliances. The corollary to this is that small companies without extensive network technology, but with a networking culture, can be more attractive partners than large companies with extensive technology but no networking culture.

In the agile world, the right alliance is a valuable commercial asset. However, how does an enterprise get to know of potential alliance partners? There may be a partner with just the right footprint somewhere, but how do we get to know of it? Networking may come to our aid. It is likely within a short period of time that preconfigured, contractual agents will be released throughout the World Wide Web. Their task will be to match possible partners based on footprint patterns. These agents can scan hundreds of thousands of web sites, far more than is possible by human means. They will make the preliminary assessment of the data and the likely suitability for an alliance.

Far-fetched? Possibly. Nonetheless, these ideas are consistent with notions of molecularization and "particle finance"[3] that has been around for some time.

4. Streamlining Approval and Review Processes

Or, agility in the processes that help you to build agility. This reminds us of the classic "bootstrapping" approach defined by networking pioneer Douglas Engelbart. First, fix the processes that help you to fix processes; this provides exponential leverage in creating capability.

Approval and review processes can be undertaken in a networked way just like any other business process. Let's ask some pertinent questions.

- Is the pro forma case of business partnering available on an intranet web page and instantly accessible across the enterprise?
- Is a profile of the intended alliance partners also available on an intranet web page?
- Has a profile of the home enterprise been made available to potential partners?
- Can alliance specialists and managers be pulled rapidly into group conferences to discuss alliance proposals without delaying for diary windows months in advance?

3. Charles S. Sanford, "Financial Markets in 2020," a paper delivered at Federal Reserve Bank of Kansas City Economic Symposium, Jackson Hole, WY, 1993, pp. 7–10.

- Is a history of the enterprise's alliance dealings available to learn from?
- When an alliance is being reviewed, can senior managers from each partner gather up-to-the-minute information about the progress of the alliance from its shared networked workspace?

Summary

An alliance doesn't make you agile, but agility employs alliances to reach out to the resources needed to enrich customers in a changing business world. Forming agile alliances means challenging certain long-held assumptions about alliances themselves. The result is a landscape of multiple alliances that are easier to form and to dissolve.

We see agile alliances in a variety of internal and external collaborations; including all "virtual organization" forms as well as cross-functional working, outsourcing, webs, and aggregators. Some of these are necessarily based on networking, all can and should be based on networking. Hence the enterprise needs agile networking capabilities to form and perform in alliances and to be an attractive alliance partner. These capabilities have to do with the networking behavior and culture of the enterprise (but not necessarily its technology), its intellectual property management, its understanding of its own profile as a partner, and its ability to approve and review alliances.

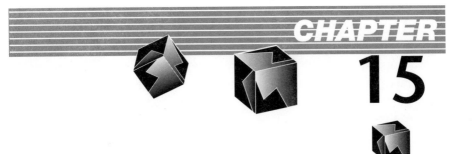

AGILE NETWORKED
COMMERCE

The new economy is a molecular economy... ."Mass" becomes "molecular" in all aspects of economic and social life.

–Don Tapscott[1]

While the intent of this book is more oriented to the "why and how" of agile networking, we do think it illustrative to offer some examples of "what" business is doing to turn networking agility to profit. Here we've drawn a few examples from various sectors of commerce, briefly describing innovations in the way things are done that are directly attributable to agile competencies sustained through networking.

A key point is that agile networking is not restricted to behind-the-scenes organizational activities. Agile networked commerce is emerging where organizations interact with markets and customers through the Internet. In this chapter we'll look at some aspects of agile networked commerce, at how organizations are using the principles of agility in the direct transaction of business with customers.

1. Don Tapscott, *The Digital Economy: Promise and Peril in the Age of Networked Intelligence* (New York: McGraw-Hill, 1996), p. 51.

Up front we should say that our purpose here is not to catalogue all the ways people have discovered to make money (or try to make money) on the Internet. Marketing, merchandising, and taking orders on the web and by email are all activities worthy of description. And, to a degree, they all involve agile networking. But our intent is to explore the fundamental aspects of agile networked commerce, not the currently hot surface phenomena. We expect that most readers are already committed to some kind of commerce. This model may provide a framework for understanding the potential of agile networking in typical areas.

Agile Commerce Model

There are three major variables in the agile commerce equation:

- The market, or customer demand
- The environment
- The enterprise

These factors are in constant change; generally, the enterprise is the dependent variable, changing in reaction to the other two. Graphically, the agile challenge to the enterprise is to maintain congruency with both the environment and the market. Figure 15–1 illustrates this calculus of agile commerce. The challenge to organizations is to sustain this congruency. In this chapter we'll look at how this is done in a few key sectors.

A final note. In the introduction to Part 4 we mentioned the trend toward molecularization, or the unbundling of commercial entities in the network to very small particles. This constitutes a span of effect of tremendous size, from the infinitely large network to the infinitely small particle or object. The power to manipulate and reconfigure particles over networks will deliver tremendous agility. And we have just seen the beginning.

Personal Services

In discussing alliances in Chapter 14 we mentioned disintermediation: the ability of a customer to electronically travel the net to the source of a service, instead of dealing through intermediaries. We've become more used to the power accruing to us as customers: we tell the doctor what pills we want, we have choices for telephone service, we call the factory to ask a question about our automobile. (There's a downside to this, too: in the United States at least, in fast-food restaurants we're asked to clear our own table trash!)

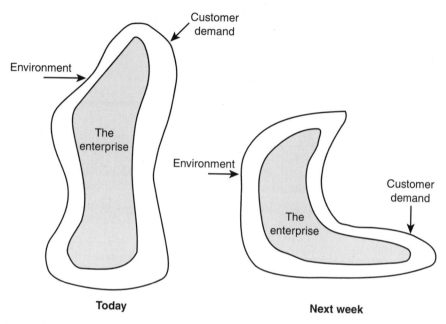

Figure 15–1 The Agile Commerce Model.

For example, late one night while on a trip we decide that we need to switch flights. In times when the rate of change was more moderate, the value of a travel agency was directly proportional to its agility in making changes for customers: providing just-in-time solutions. But change happens so fast now that the mere fact that the agency is only a stop on the mainline to that solution takes it out of the running. Instead of going through the travel agent, we call the airline or get on line to the airline web site to make the change. No need to wake up an intermediary. The network provides the medium for the agile solution: the flight, the class, the seat, the payment are all handled at the source.

Of course, as we saw in Chapter 14, agile competitors can up the ante by becoming aggregators in this kind of situation. An apt example is Microsoft's Expedia™, a service offered over the web that enables you to make all your travel arrangements. This is the electronic travel bureau: not just the transportation, but the hotel, restaurants, and recreational activities. This provides you a total solution, one-stop shopping, without the need for an intermediary.

Information Services

We had an adventurous acquaintance whose motto was "anything worth doing is worth doing to excess." That's okay as long as no one suffers the consequences. Consumers today complain of too much information. Yogi Berra, a colorful baseball player of past decades once remarked about a nightclub, "That place is so crowded that nobody goes there anymore." We've talked to more than one manager who laments that he or she gets so much email that they no longer even try to read it.

This problem for consumers is recognized as an opportunity by agile networked businesses, who provide ways of focusing information on the networks to suit individual customer's needs. The solutions offered range everywhere, from software filters that help to sort your mail, to information services that send you only the kinds of information that you'd be interested in. At the high end of the latter are emerging services that allege to watch what you do on the net, learn what you really want to know, and link you to sites that can provide that kind of information. Given past experience, we suspect the fine hand of marketing involvement here, but will withhold judgment.

The kinds of information services that we think are most agile, though, are access rather than distribution based. Of course, the World Wide Web is a kind of information service; so are America Online® and Compuserve®. At a more focused and expensive level are on-line services like Mainspring™. Mainspring links a wide network of knowledge experts and published information together with people who need specific knowledge in leading-edge areas of enterprise: on-line security, virtual teaming, and emerging standards, for example.

We know that access-based information solutions are clearly better suited to connecting people with what they want to know without the tremendous overhead of what they don't need to know. Witness the tremendous interest in "Frequently Asked Questions" sections of web sites. Conventional wisdom says that 80% of what people want to know can be directly accessed through the Q&A mode; they do not have to dig it out of a long document. In communication, anything beyond what you need is noise, and noise degrades the message.

The "unbundling" or molecularization we mentioned earlier in the chapter is evident here. Facilities such as the web and hypertext have made it possible to access information in smaller and smaller particles. Why search through 10 reports when a few figures is all you need? Information services are learning how to link semantically related bits of information and retrieve them on customer request. The customer pays for the value of the information retrieved, not the publisher's price for a set of documents.

The Electronic Storefront

The most visible symbol of the power of networking and agility is the electronic, or digital, storefront. This is most often a web site but can also be an interconnected system of groupware applications.[2] The electronic storefront can manage everything from initial customer discovery of a commercial (or other) offering to the ultimate electronic shipping of a product. Of course, the full-cycle model is best practiced by software developers, whose products live on the network. Supplier's on-line sites, as well as those of distributors, do everything from persuading you that you need an application to downloading the product in exchange for your credit card number, sending you updates, and having a library of fixes for future bugs and viruses. By adding a site to your web browser bookmarks, you're never very far from the store: life in the electronic mall.

But this is a two-way street. Just as information services can sense your needs through the network, so can vendors of all kinds of products and services. Living in the mall can have drawbacks, not the least of which is constant exposure to very tempting ways to spend your money. The network does not forget. Buy a trout fly this week and for many months your mailbox will be filled with once-in-a-lifetime fishing gear offers. Just for you. Exactly what you've always wanted.

And even possessing a web site or contributing to a newsgroup can make you the target for unsolicited emails for products serving an alarmingly wide spectrum of human activity. One of us recently received an unsolicited email from a company who was selling software to ensure that email advertisements only went to people who had solicited them.

Interacting with the Customer

One of the key agile strategies is collaborative development of products through interaction with the customer. There's nothing new in this, but it

2. Andrew Dahl and Leslie Lesnik, *Internet Commerce* (Indianapolis, IN: New Riders Publishing, 1996), p. 209.

did get forgotten for a time. In olden days, the squire went to the carpenter in the village, they discussed what the squire wanted, and the carpenter built it. Then along came mass production, and for nearly 100 years we've been increasingly offered one-size-fits-all products. Agility points out that this is no longer a sustainable source of competitive advantage, for a number of reasons to do with global competition and market segmentation. One added, new reason is the impact of the Internet on the ability to interact with customers.

Ubiquitous communication through the Internet has enabled private, individual customers to participate in the design of the products that they want. This ranges from design by selection to full design input. Using the World Wide Web and its graphical capabilities, customers can

- Select from the much greater range of products that can be displayed on the web than in the local store.
- Select customization features of products viewed virtually: for example color, trim, and accessories for automobiles.
- Detail full design specifications, for example in fashion clothing.

And the impact is not only for physical product.

- Financial services companies mount sophisticated questionnaires on web forms as the front end to tailoring a solution directly for the individual.
- We've spoken of travel already, but we point out here that many travel aggregators' business relies on web-based interaction with the customer, designing the desired itinerary.
- On-line newspapers are now offering readers the chance to design a personalized edition that highlights topics that they have said they want to read about. Premium on-line information services are already offering this.
- Through Internet interaction, customers of software companies can order very specific combinations of functionality, national language, platform, and licensing option (molecularization, to some degree) and have the software delivered electronically.

Marketing professionals are identifying a dramatic new phenomenon in this interactive business. Rather than mass advertising—producing one advertisement for populations—the Internet allows tailored marketing messages to be developed for smaller and smaller groups. Sounds like molecularization again? You got it. And how do you know about these groups and what marketing messages will be meaningful to them? Because you get them to fill in questionnaires on your web site before they get access to the products that they're seeking. So mass marketing is going the way of mass production. The customer is being recognized as an individual. Once again, an agile strategy is accelerated by Internet connectivity.

And notice what's happening here. The consumer is no longer the passive recipient of marketing material through the media, billboards, and fliers. He or she is actively coming to your web site out of interest. One thing you know about anyone who crosses your URL threshold is that he or she is interested in what you have to offer. But, as they say in consulting, the minute you sign a customer, you start to lose them. While the relationship starts when the mouse clicks, so does the potential downward slide of customer interest. The new battleground will be keeping customers' interest in your site—keeping them coming back so that you can form a relationship with them. The agile enterprise will learn increasingly sophisticated ways to maintain customer interest with attractive, changing content and collateral material and services that do not have to be directly related to the product being offered: for example, daily cartoons, pungent quotes, prize competitions, special offers, discussion forums, new productivity tools, and the like.

A final point that shows the penetration of customer interaction. Customers are even now contributing to company product support. What are "Frequently Asked Questions" web pages but the result of a customer's helping a company to support its product?

Intellectual Property

[c]opyright should . . . be understood as a divisible bundle of rights that may be allocated among different parties to provide maximum opportunities for sharing and learning.[3]

3. Consortium for Educational Technology for University Systems, "Ownership of New Works at the University: Unbundling of Rights and the Pursuit of Higher Learning" (Long Beach, CA: Trustees of California State University, 1997).

A key challenge in networked commerce is keeping track of intellectual property: who "owns" what bit of information for how long. And just as important, how do you get revenue from users of the information? Bits get smaller every day, recombinations get more ingenious, and access continues to spread. It becomes more and more difficult to work out who should be paid for what. In short, the problem will get worse before it gets better.

Let's just remind ourselves that intellectual property issues are of particular importance to the agile enterprise. Agile enterprises are knowledge based and tend to sell knowledge products or goods with high knowledge ratios. However, just when agility is requiring more attention to commercial return on intellectual property, networking is requiring a review of established practices.

We offer no succor. There are a wide range of perspectives on the issue of intellectual property in the network. At one end of the scale there are those who don't see the qualitative differences in how intellectual property is handled in the network, only questions of size and speed.[4] At the other extreme is the view that the whole game has changed because of networking. The implication is that agility in the way users access information will need to be matched with agility in the way rights are protected, that ownership rights break down when information (text, music, art) go digital.[5] In the middle are views that intellectual property legislation should apply more widely than at present, but be more limited, pay fair shares to all, but not exclude follow-on exploitation.[6]

Finance

We all know about on-line banking, from the anonymous ATM, to our local bank, to the megabanks and on-line services. All can serve you better on line. Networks are ideal media for financial dealings. Numbers fly back and forth across the net just as easily as does software. They unbundle easily; ones and zeros make fine particles. And the speed of transac-

---

4. Howard Hill, "Lawyers: Current Laws Will Work in Cyberspace," *Sacramento Gazette*, Vol. 2, August 1, 1997.

5. John Perry Barlow, "Selling Wine without Bottles: The Economy of Mind in the Global Net" (1993). Available from the web site of The Electronic Frontier Foundation.

6. John Kay, "The Myth of Intellectual Property," *Demos Quarterly*, Issue 8, 1996.

tion is the banker's friend; it helps to obviate the bill payer's last resort: float.[7] Here we'll look at another aspect of financial commerce, again dealing with that intriguing combination of networks and very small objects: particle finance.

The concept of particle finance first came to our attention in a paper by Charles S. Sanford, chairman of the board, Bankers Trust Company.[8] He explains that artifacts such as securities are usually valued (or their risk assessed) as aggregated bundles. Through the power of networks, links can be maintained to the sources of all the particles that form the bundle, creating a much more specific accounting of value and risk. Factors can be noted in real time. Sanford notes such factors as "financial market volatility, changes in global product, the volumes of our transaction processing, an earthquake in Japan, changes in consumer confidence in the United Kingdom, or a change in our corporate strategy."[9] By any definition, this qualifies as networking agility, perhaps not affecting us directly as consumers, but surely making an impact on our investments and pensions.

An anecdote from the Far East illustrates the precision of the network–particle model. At a hotel in Kuala Lumpur, Malaysia, weary business people stand at the bar sipping their vodka tonics. A display over the bar continually flashes a set of numbers. It is calculating in real time the "cost" of the drink based on the current price of the ingredients. We can imagine the discussions over who got the best deal.

Conclusion

These glimpses of the contributions that agile networking is making to new forms of commerce are intended to be suggestive, but not exhaustive. What they suggest is the synergy between agility and Internet-based commerce.

7. One banking network noted that through 24-hour banking it eliminated float, saving $1 billion per year: just-in-time banking. Example cited in Geoff J. Mulgan, *Communication and Control: Networks and the New Economics of Communication* (New York: Guilford Press, 1991), p. 235–7.

8. Charles S. Sanford, "Financial Markets in 2020," a paper delivered at Federal Reserve Bank of Kansas City Economic Symposium, Jackson Hole, WY, 1993, pp. 7–10. Note also that immediacy and internetworking are two of Tapscott's "Twelve Themes of the New Economy," *The Digital Economy*, Chapter 2.

9. Sanford, p. 8.

Agility didn't invent the Internet. Indeed, when the initial agility research was being conducted in 1991–1992, the Internet was an interesting but specialist tool. It wasn't until 1993 that the Internet took off due to World Wide Web protocols and user-friendly graphical browsers. Since then there's been an accelerating crosstalk between agility's message and the capabilities that the Internet offers.

Most of this crosstalk has been positive for agility. The network is driving enterprises toward agile behavior, whether that is explicitly recognized or not. It's increasingly setting an agile context.

CHAPTER

16

AGILE NETWORKED EDUCATION

I'll tell you what distance learning is to me. Distance learning is when I have to leave my house to go to a class.

—A thoroughly modern California State University student.

Virtuality and agility strongly imply crossing boundaries to get a job done. Virtual organizations are made up of competencies that transcend cultural, and geographic boundaries. They are virtually one, but, in reality, many. Agility demands crossing boundaries to enrich customers and respond to change.

One boundary that continues to resist crossing is that between business and education, one of the most durable "us and them" dichotomies in history. But this wall, too, shows signs of cracking.

- As described in Chapter 10, visionaries like Bill Olson of Hewlett– Packard see through the false curtain and strive to integrate learning with work.
- Recently, we've seen the rise of corporate universities embracing modern networking delivery technologies and aspiring to go beyond the mind-set of corporate training departments.
- Businesses constantly team with universities and independent specialists to meet training and learning needs.

We've already discussed agile learning in the corporate environment in Chapter 11. It is with some reluctance that we dedicate a separate chapter to institutional "education" as though it were a land apart from the world of business. But, regretfully, it remains so. Going back to the means-and-ends argument of Chapter 13, we see educational institutions as a means to an end: learning. But many institutions have becomes ends in themselves. The issues separating business and education are not about learning as much as they are about the establishments themselves: industrial and academic bureaucracies. The implication here is that universities that focus on learning rather than on themselves can break through these boundaries and develop new value-adding services.

In this chapter we'll illustrate how agile networking pertains in the world of education. We focus on a single public university system, the California State University (CSU). CSU understands the need to be agile in the future and has set about building agile networking capabilities. Granted, other kinds of universities could be used as the subject.

- Corporate universities and institutes capture the learning within their organizations and offer it to stakeholders. The Arthur D. Little School of Management, Motorola University, and Sun Virtual University are well respected members of the genre.
- For-profit universities, such as the University of Phoenix, who are extremely agile in matching instructional competencies to market needs, hiring adjunct faculty to quickly make new courses available at campuses through the country.
- Open universities and community colleges that also provide essential learning services.

We've chosen CSU for a couple of reasons. First, they are just embarking on an initiative that enables us to see an agile networking design as it gets underway, rather than in retrospect. Second, theirs is not just a product focus: degrees, programs, and courses. Rather, they realize that educational enterprises are organizations just as much as Kodak or Boeing or Hewlett–Packard is an organization. Finally, CSU knows it needs to address agility at all levels: governance, markets, customers, delivery systems, management and support processes, teams and contributors, and technology.

A final introductory note. We'll structure this last chapter in a way that brings us full circle from Part 1. After a short overview, we'll use the principles of agility to organize the agile networking aspects of the CSU initiative. This will give us a unified picture of networking agility that is applicable, we think, in many organizational settings. Perhaps it will be another small step in crossing the boundaries between the worlds of business and education.

The Situation

The California State University system consists of 23 campus-based institutions located in both rural and urban areas throughout California. In California's tiered approach to education, the campuses focus primarily on upper-level undergraduate and graduate-level courses and degrees. Currently, the system has over 300,000 students enrolled. Historically, the campuses of the system have had a fair amount of autonomy, with the freedom to be entrepreneurial and to offer the kinds of programs that meet the needs in their areas. Several campuses have been innovative in distance learning, which has begun to blur regional distinctions.

System-level governance comes largely out of the Chancellor's Office in Long Beach. Over time, system-wide programs have been initiated, some with success, some not. But a recent program, initiated in 1996 by the Chancellor's Office, called the deal on the future challenges the university faced. Named *Cornerstones*,[1] this perspective was the collaborative effort of a system-wide team of faculty and administrators. It addressed head on the issues of unavoidable change and offered guidelines for the university to build the capabilities requisite to agilely manage the future.

Cornerstones contained four nonnegotiable tenets:

- Highest standards of undergraduate education
- Increasing student access while maintaining the current resource levels
- Being accountable across university functions
- Being poised to respond to continuing change

---

1. Molly Corbett Broad and others, "Cornerstones: Planning for the Next Decade, Draft Report" (Long Beach, CA: California State University Office of the Chancellor, March 1997).

To prepare them for the predicted and predictable future, the system and campuses launched a number of action-based initiatives aimed at implementing Cornerstones.

Forces of Change

Like Scrooge's three ghosts, the changes challenging the CSU dwell in the past, present, and future. Not much can be done about the past, except to learn from it, but the present and future offer opportunities, or threats, demanding action.

Past changes affecting the CSU were large economic. As a result of voter tax rebellion, funding for the university was at best fixed, possibly diminishing. The cost of a CSU education is about three times what students pay in tuition, and state funding is based on enrollment. Less state funding means less enrollment, a deadly spiral. Also, student demographics has changed. The average age of students had risen steadily, at some campuses to 27 to 28 years. As long ago as 1990, we were told that the modal student at one CSU campus was a 27-year-old working mother.

Currently, the pressures of economics and changing student needs continue. More and more students are working full time. Many are unable to travel to campuses because of work, child care, or other constraining circumstances. Continuing education and training are now life long needs for individuals. An expanded student population seeks services in diverse ways, including ways of accessing education while avoiding the time and place limitations of on-campus instruction.

The future seems to hold more of the same, with a kicker. A demographic phenomenon known as Tidal Wave II is expected to bring over 100,000 new students into the state system over the next few years. Further demand will arise as new generations within certain minority groups pursue further education. According to Cornerstones, meeting the needs of California's learners will require dramatic changes in the way education is delivered, all with little or no increase in state funding.

Where all these challenges converged was in the notion of somehow providing more economical access to learning by more students while maintaining high levels of quality. Clearly this involved distance learning—perhaps a virtual university.

The Gap

In most organizations, academia not excepted, there is a real gap between espoused policy and operational reality. The exigencies of time, budget, culture, new management, old habits, and the Next Great Policy often sound the death knell for apparently good directions. Middle management was supposed to effect new policies, but was usually to busy surviving and more recently has been downsized to below critical mass. So how do good ideas like Cornerstones become realized? In the academic community it certainly isn't by top-down mandate. Rather, it takes building a community that includes all stakeholders, including faculty, staff, students, legislators, private citizens, and potential students.

This is how CSU approached implementation: the consensus approach. We bring this up because, while agility and its attributes may make sense to some of us, there are constituencies who don't see the point. And they cannot be ignored.

Enriching the Customer

To many faculty, used to the values, autonomy, and security of traditional education, it is not intuitive that the student is a customer. Nor is competition for students something that professors consider on a daily basis. There's just so much room on campus, a cohort of students enrolls, classes fill up, and we're off to another semester. Occasionally, courses don't "make," but there's usually an overload somewhere else to make up for that inconvenience.

But a sea change is coming to academia under a variety of names, like "outcomes assessment." To oversimplify, this means that it's not enough to measure the quality of education by surveying the faculty, the classrooms, the books in the library, and the course catalogue. Instead, you need to look at what students have learned: the outcomes. This focus on outcomes rather than processes is itself driven by networking. In a connected world, customers can buy services from anywhere, not limited by geographical proximity. Potential university students are no different. The complexity caused by thousands of network-wide programs and courses means that students will increasingly assess offerings by reference to the quality of outcomes.

This obviates the old saw: "I taught them, but they didn't learn." The learner is the customer, and the value of the learning transaction is determined by how the learning outcome enriches the student. The value of the service is determined by the recipient, not the provider. And in this case the end recipient may not be the student so much as the eventual employer.

In a collateral initiative, CSU is accelerating its efforts to learn from businesses what they see as educational needs in California, through customer focus groups of business leaders.

Once we see the learner as customer, the idea of competition is easier to take, especially when technology enables learning institutions to beam their programs and courses anywhere in the world. Individual CSU campuses, long used to a "no poaching" policy in their regions, now find that they can offer courses to each other's students through the Internet. Worse than that, anyone can offer courses to their students by wire. Out of state, even out of country, education providers can reach into traditional geographically based markets.

Nor is physical competition excluded. A dean at an upstate campus remarked that no one was much concerned about competition until a sign for the University of Phoenix went up across the street. Phoenix operates very agilely on-line, but also out of storefronts, using adjunct faculty with full-time jobs in the fields in which they teach. As adjuncts, they receive no benefits and cost about one-fourth as much as full-time faculty. Combine that with minimal campus expenses and you get a very strong competitor: high quality, low cost, no frills.

So how to compete for customers? CSU's Fresno campus had a good idea. They noticed that the California's state expenditures for prisons were rising, this year intersecting the downward trend of expenditures for education. Rather than complain about this reality, Fresno developed a program for delivering degree and certification programs to corrections officers at the prison workplace. The original plan was to use in-place analogue downlinks for satellite video course delivery. But it turned out that shift scheduling made synchronous learning sessions near impossible. So the switch was made to videotapes. And plans are underway for web-based learning.

Distance isn't the point; access is. Customers can't be expected to want to come to campus anymore, even if they live or work across the street. So the agile learning provider uses the network to deliver to the customer site.

Leveraging Resources

We've already mentioned the importance of recognizing the university culture. The essential core competency of the university system is represented in its faculty. Winning faculty support for any new direction, especially a system-level effort, would not be easy. Faculty are rightly suspicious of new organizational units, and talk of a "virtual university" brought forth visions of yet another level of bureaucracy.

And there was such talk. Indeed, from as high up as the governor's office, directives were flying about that suggested a statewide "virtual university." Chuck Lindahl, the vice-chancellor, was the person "managing the gap." He was responsible for evolving CSU's systemic capabilities to cope with the future. Realizing the resistance and confusion surrounding "virtual university," he decided to drop the organizational fixation and concentrate on capabilities. Thus was born an initiative to develop CSU's Distributed Learning Services. This sent all the right signals: a system-wide effort to provide access to the product—learning—to customers wherever they might be.[2]

Components of the CSU's Distributed Learning Services were existing or nearly existing resources leveraged for this new agile purpose, as follows.

System Resources

The heart of this new learning service would be the network. CSU already had CSUnet, a robust, system-wide "intranet" that connected all campuses. In addition, all campuses had two-way video, or CODEC systems, that could be used for either meetings or classes. Tom West, CSU's VP of information systems had already put in place a *Baselines* program through which the system helped to bring all campuses up to a basic level of technical capability. This involved computerization, network access, and training.

System-level resources were also to be called in to provide marketing and coordination. When nine campuses offered web-based courses during

2. Notice how, after initial faltering, CSU rejected the idea of a departmental approach in favor of a learning services approach. This exactly parallels the transition we recommend in corporate environments from a "training department" to "provider of agile learning services." The customer-value-enriching philosophy of agility naturally produces the change in focus from "entity" to "service."

the summer of 1997, a single-system web site provided the unified catalogue for prospective students.

Finally, it became an article of faith that the technology and support
infrastructure would serve all constituencies in the system. Courseware
and support activities would all use the network. Academic support activities for face-to-face students would also offer the same services to distance
students. Everyone in the community would be a first-class citizen.

Campus Resources

As the intranet began making it easier to cross campus boundaries, the
campuses became more aware of expertise at the various sites. Some campuses were already producing excellent distance learning programs and
courses. CSU Dominguez Hills, south of Los Angeles, had a widely praised
nursing course and web-based MBA. CSU Chico was already using existing satellite communications to reach over 40 industrial customers. CSU
Long Beach had excellent facilities for designing and testing the usability
of web-based, asynchronous courseware. A new spirit of cooperation
arose as campuses began calling on each other's expertise, seeing centers
of relevant competency instead of budgetary rivals.

Information

Use of the web and interlinked home pages provided instantaneous access
to information about the Distance Learning Services initiative. All new
efforts were disseminated on the web and discussed through email listserv-
ers. Stakeholders located across California were invited in to see in real
time what was happening in projects, instead of waiting for an ultimate
"report." People soon discovered that real-time, on-line feedback was
much more effective than the traditional presentation and gripe session
approach.

Cooperating to Compete

As potential markets for CSU's Distributed Learning Services were discovered, a few things became clear. The demand was more for programs than
for courses. Virtual offerings would not be one-off faculty favorites, but
rather well thought out clusters that would lead to a skill, certification or
degree. It made sense, therefore, for campuses to collaborate in offering

programs. Given that the focus was the customer, not the campus, thinking about "my students" shifts to "our learners." Rather than worrying about losing a student to another campus, campuses focused on bringing new students and revenue into the system.

The larger cooperation issues lie, however, outside the system. Will campuses form network learning alliances with external learning providers? With other universities, businesses, or consultancies? Logic says things will go this way, and odds are that cross-boundary educational alliances will proliferate.

Mastering Change

The heaviest charge placed on the system by the campuses in this program has been for leadership and agility (okay, and money). One full professor actually used the term "inertial processes" to describe the glacial speed at which some issues were handled through the system. While they revere the considered approach, many faculty, however, realize the urgent need to eliminate the sluggishness of basic processes. Agility does not equate to carelessness or the slighting of the learning process. On the contrary, it is key to the university of the future's meeting the new and ever changing learning challenges of its customers.

Thus the CSU system is revisiting and redesigning processes to make them more agile: marketing, on-line registration, system-wide library access, electronic "one card" access to resources, and management of credits and charges from multiple campuses. Many of these elements are grounded in the premise of network rather than physical access.

Moreover, the future perspective is helping CSU to master change. Currently, the practical implementation of Distributed Learning Services in full roll-out is still in the future. All CSU can do, and what it is doing and what it should do, is to put in place capabilities that can accommodate the varieties of educational process that it will be called on to provide. Thus, rather than defining structures and processes (whats), it is operating agilely to build capabilities (hows).

We can see this focus on capabilities rather than events again in CSU's approach to its technology infrastructure. CSU management decided to take the agile high road in technology development. Building on current infrastructure, they rolled out a balanced technology plan that would accommodate whatever market demands there would be for educational products. This mean investing in—some thought "taking a flier on"—various technologies: a high-speed T3 network to replace CSUnet and a network that would include future customer downlink sites, the 180 California community colleges. Taking a future perspective, CSU technology leaders plan not to be surprised by future demands on its infrastructure.

Some questions remain. Will courseware be modularized enough to allow reconfiguration of modules from different partners to meet suddenly emerging learning needs? How many faculty will acquire the new skills to offer courses in the networked environment? What future demands will students have of their education system? Whatever the answers, CSU has made a fine start to meeting the agile education needs of the future.

Conclusion

CSU's program contains many hallmarks of agility. It's noteworthy, however, that, outside key program leaders, agility isn't today a word in common parlance in the CSU. We see agility in what CSU is doing and have reported so in this chapter. But to the people involved the changes underway are a natural response to the way the education world is changing, particularly because of the impact of networking.

As we close this book this point is worth highlighting. Agility—a strategy of strategies for being competitive in conditions of change—increasingly seems simply the natural way to go. It seems the natural way to go because agility emerged as a coherent response to the changes taking place in the real world. There's no reason to be surprised when the real world spontaneously develops agile initiatives. What we can do is to help organizations to capitalize on those initiatives by introducing them to the rich, coherent picture of agility.

BIBLIOGRAPHY

Ackoff, Russell L., *Management in Small Doses.* New York: John Wiley & Sons, Inc., 1986.

Agility Forum, *Key Need Areas for Integrating the Virtual Enterprise.* Bethlehem, PA: The Agility Forum, Report AR94-04, 1994.

—, "Change Domains," (videotape). Bethlehem, PA.: The Agility Forum, 1995.

—, "People Development Group Newsletter." Bethlehem, PA.: Iacocca Institute, February 1996.

Alexander, Christopher, Sara Ishikawa and Murray Silverstein, "The Web of Public Transportation," in *A Pattern Language: Towns, Buildings, Construction,* ed. Alexander, Ishikawa, and Silverstein, p. 94. New York: Oxford University Press, 1977.

Barlow, John Perry, "Selling Wine without Bottles: The Economy of Mind in the Global Net," (1993). Available from the web site of The Electronic Frontier Foundation.

Basarab, David J., Sr., and Darrell K. Root, *The Training Evaluation Process.* Boston: Kluwer, 1992.

Broad, Molly Corbett, and others, "Cornerstones: Planning for the Next Decade, Draft Report." Long Beach, CA.: California State University Office of the Chancellor, March 1997.

Business Week, "The Top Managers of 1995," August 1, 1996.

Consortium for Educational Technology for University Systems, "Ownership of New Works at the University: Unbundling of Rights and the Pursuit of Higher Learning." Long Beach, CA.: Trustees of California State University, 1997.

Dahl, Andrew, and Leslie Lesnick, *Internet Commerce* , p. 209. Indianapolis, IN: New Riders Publishing, 1996.

Davis, Stan, and Jim Botkin, *The Monster under the Bed: How Business is Mastering the Opportunity of Knowledge for Profit.* New York: Simon and Schuster, 1994.

Dove, Rick, "Agile Supply Chain Management" *Automotive Production*, April 1996.

Gilmore, James H., and B. Joseph Pine II, "Customization—The Four Faces," *Harvard Business Review,* January–February 1997, pp. 91–101.

Goldman, Steven L., and Kenneth Preiss, (eds.), Roger N. Nagel and Rick Dove (principal investigators), *21st Century Manufacturing Enterprise Strategy: An Industry-Led View.* Bethlehem, PA.: Iacocca Institute Lehigh University, 1991.

—, Roger N. Nagel, and Kenneth Preiss, *Agile Competitors and Virtual Organizations.* New York: Van Nostrand Reinhold, 1995.

Grenier, Ray, and George Metes, *Enterprise Networking: Working Together Apart.* Maynard, MA.: Digital Press, 1992.

— and —, *Going Virtual*, Chapter 18. Upper Saddle River, NJ: Prentice Hall PTR, 1995.

Grimes & Battersby, "Valuation of Intellectual Property," pp. 208–211. Stamford, CT.: Grimes & Battersby, Spring 1993.

Gunneson, Alvin O., *Transitioning to Agility.* Reading, MA: Addison-Wesley, 1997.

Handy, Charles, *Beyond Certainty.* London: Arrow Books Ltd., 1996.

Hague, Douglas, "The Firm as University," *Demos Quarterly,* Issue 8, 1996.

Hill, Howard, "Lawyers: Current Laws Will Work in Cyberspace," *Sacramento Gazette,* Vol. 2, August 1, 1997.

Hiltz, Starr Roxanne, "Collaborative Learning in a Virtual Classroom," in *Proceedings of the Conference on Computer-supported Cooperative Work 1988, Portland, Oregon* , pp. 282–290. New York: Association for Computing Machinery, Inc., 1988.

Hope, Tony, and Jeremy Hope, *Transforming the Bottom Line.* London: Nicholas Brealey Publishing, 1995.

Johnson, David, and Roger Johnson, "What We Know about Cooperative Learning at the College Level," *Cooperative Learning,* 13, no. 3, (1993).

Kalish, David K., "Apple's Enemies Have Reason to Save It," *New Hampshire Sunday News,* August 10, 1997, p. D–1.

Katzenbach, Jon R., and Douglas K. Smith, *The Wisdom of Teams.* Boston: Harvard Business School Press, 1993.

Kay, John, "The Myth of Intellectual Property," *Demos Quarterly*, Issue 8, 1996.

Labich, Kenneth, "Why Companies Fail," *Fortune*, November 14, 1994.

Lipnack, Jessica, and Jeffrey Stamps, *The Teamnet Factor: Bringing the Power of Boundary Crossing into the Heart of Your Business*. Essex Junction, VT: Oliver Wight, 1993.

— and —, *Virtual Teams: Reaching across Space, Time and Organizations with Technology*. New York: John Wiley & Sons, Inc., 1997.

Manville, Brook, and Nathaniel Foote, "Strategy As If Knowledge Mattered," *Fast Company*, April/May 1996.

— and —, "Harvest Your Workers' Knowledge," *Datamation*, July, 1996.

McGrath, Joseph E., *Groups: Interaction And Performance*. Englewood Cliffs, NJ: Prentice Hall, 1984.

McRae, Hamish, *The World in 2020*. New York: HarperCollins, 1994.

Morrison, Ian, *The Second Curve: Managing the Velocity of Change*. New York: Ballantine Books, 1996.

Mulgan, Geoff J., *Communication and Control: Networks and the New Economics of Communication*, pp. 235–7. New York, Guilford Press, 1991.

Nagel, Roger, and Rick Dove, *21st Century Manufacturing Enterprise Strategy*. Bethlehem, PA.: Iacocca Institute, Lehigh University, 1991.

Nonaka, Ikujiro, and Hirotaka Takeuchi, *The Knowledge-creating Company: How Japanese Companies Create the Dynamics of Innovation*. Oxford: Oxford University Press, 1995.

Perelman, Lewis J., *School's Out: Hyperlearning, the New Technology, and the End of Education*. New York: William Morrow and Co., Inc., 1992.

Preiss, Kenneth, Steven L. Goldman, and Roger N. Nagel, *Cooperate to Compete*. New York: Van Nostrand Reinhold, 1996.

Quinn, James Bryan, *Intelligent Enterprise: A Knowledge and Service Based Paradigm for Industry*. New York: Macmillan,1992.

Reitman, Jerry L., *Beyond 2000: The Future of Direct Marketing*. Lincolnwood, IL.: NTC Business Books, 1994.

Ryan, Bernard, *The Corporate Intranet: Create and Manage an Internal Web for Your Organization*. New York: John Wiley & Sons, Inc., 1996.

Sanford, Charles S., "Financial Markets in 2020," pp. 7–10, a paper delivered at Federal Reserve Bank of Kansas City Economic Symposium, Jackson Hole, WY, 1993.

Schutte, Jerald G., "Virtual Teaching in Higher Education," unpublished paper, Department of Sociology, California State University Northridge, California, 1997.

Senge, Peter, *The Fifth Discipline.* New York: Doubleday/Currency, 1990.

Shelton, Ken (ed.), *In Search of Quality.* Provo, UT: Executive Excellence Publishing, 1995.

Sperling, John, and Robert W. Tucker, *For Profit Higher Education: Developing a World-class Workforce.* New Brunswick, N.J.: Transaction Publishers, 1996.

Sproull, Lee, and Sara Kiesler, *Connections.* Boston: The MIT Press, 1991.

Tapscott, Don, *The Digital Economy: Promise and Peril in the Age of Networked Intelligence* , p. 51. New York: McGraw-Hill, 1996.

Western Interstate Commission for Higher Education, "When Distance Education Crosses State Boundaries: Western States' Policies." Boulder, CO: The Commission, 1995.

Whitehead, Alfred North, *Science and the Modern World,* p. 175. New York: Macmillan, 1925.

Wolff, Leon, *In Flanders Fields—The 1917 Campaign,* p. 239. New York: Ballantine Books, 1958.

Zack, Michael H., and Michael Serino, *Knowledge Management and Collaboration Technologies.* Cambridge, MA: Lotus Development Corporation, 1996.

INDEX

America Online, 222
Anonymity, 90
Apple, 210
Arthur D. Little School of Management, 230
Attention economy, 30, 107
Audioconferencing:
    agile ECO process in, 142
    agile learning tool as, 161, 162
    collaborative learning and, 166

—B—

Barlow, John Perry, 214
Ben Franklin Institute of Technology, 211
Berra, Yogi, 222
Best practices networks:
    agile program teams and, 145
    agility and, 146
    energy company example, 147–48
    virtual university example, 148–50
Bullitt, 8
Business Week, 10, 11

—C—

California State University:
    best practices network, 148–50, 230–38
    Chancellor's Office, 231
    change forces, 232
    Chico, 236
    Chuck Lindahl, 235
    cooperating to compete, 236–37
    Cornerstones policy, 231–33
    CSUnet, 235, 238
    Distributed Learning Services, 235–37
    Dominguez Hills, 236
    enriching the customer, 233–35
    Fresno, 234

leveraging resources, 235–36
Long Beach, 236
mastering change, 237–38
purpose restating, 73
Tom West, 235
virtual university, 234
CD–ROM, 159
Change:
    agile change domains, 59–65
    agile change proficiency assessment, 63–64
    agile change proficiency domains, 61–63
    California State University at, 232
    continuous, 23
    embracing, 38–40
    mastering, 35–40
    opportunity and, 38–39
    proficiency function, 39
    today's business environment, 5–6
    unpredictability, 7
Coaching, 172, 190, 198
Collaboration with customer:
    enriching the customer and, 32
    group communication and, 86
    Internet and, 223–25
Collaborative learning, 163–66
Commitment:
    agility and, 25
    group communication and, 87–89
    leveraging resources and, 44
    open communication and, 90
Communication (*See also* Group communication *and* Open communication):
    flow, 44, 90
    group, 77–93
Community, 49
Community of practice, 119, 126